D0446774

I

REALLY

DIDN'T

THINK

THIS

THROUGH

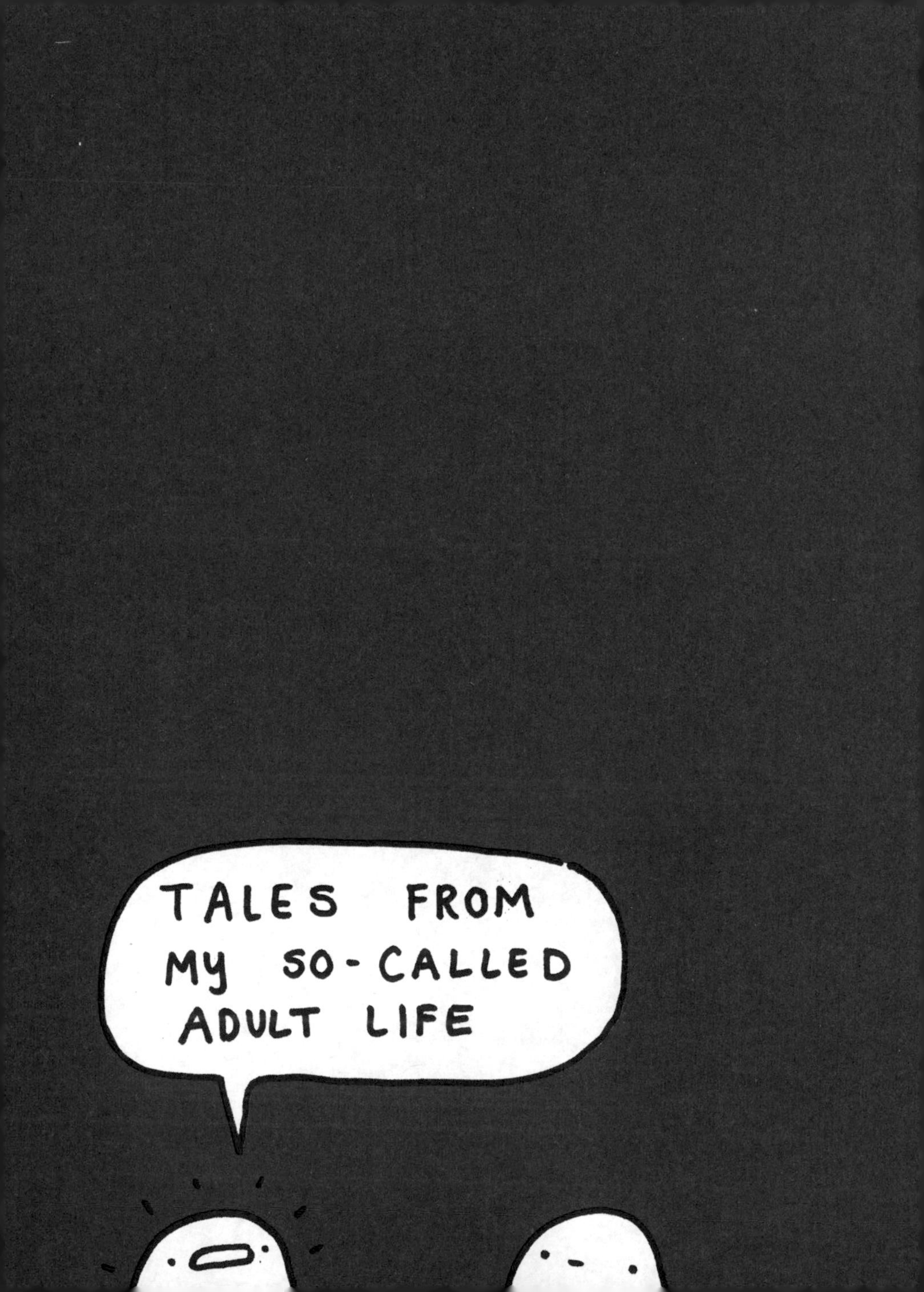
TALES FROM MY SO-CALLED ADULT LIFE

I REALLY DIDN'T THINK THIS THROUGH

by

BETH EVANS

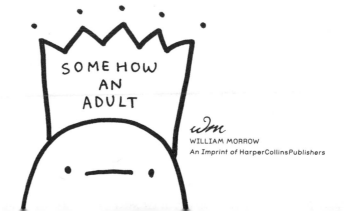

SOMEHOW
AN
ADULT

WILLIAM MORROW
An Imprint of HarperCollinsPublishers

HarperCollins books may be purchased for educational, business, or sales promotional use. For information, please email the Special Markets Department at SPsales@harpercollins.com.

FIRST EDITION

Library of Congress Cataloging-in-Publication Data has been applied for.

ISBN 978-0-06-279606-6

18 19 20 21 22 LSC 10 9 8 7 6 5 4 3 2 1

For everyone who has read my work over the years—thank you for changing my life

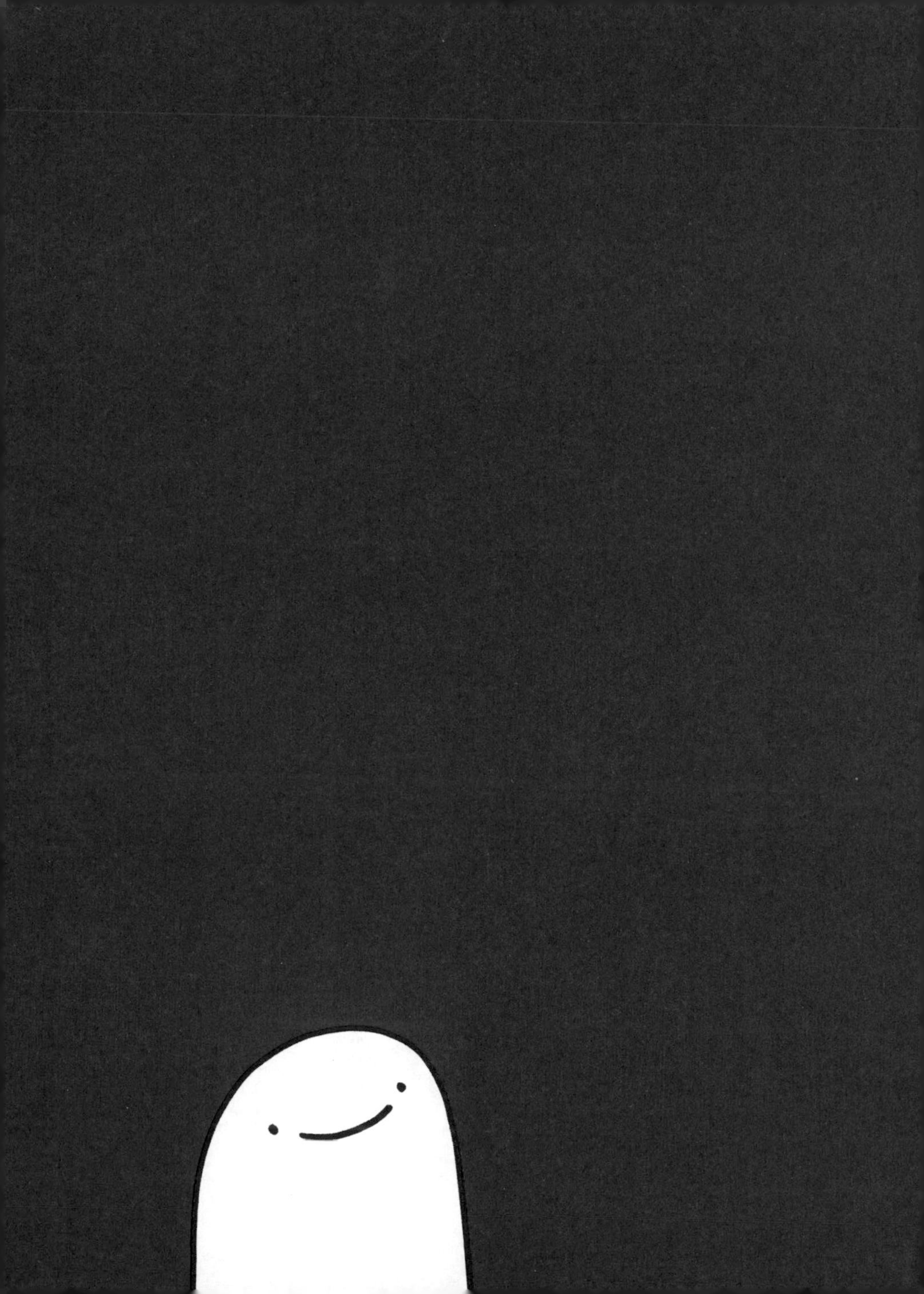

Contents

CONTENTS

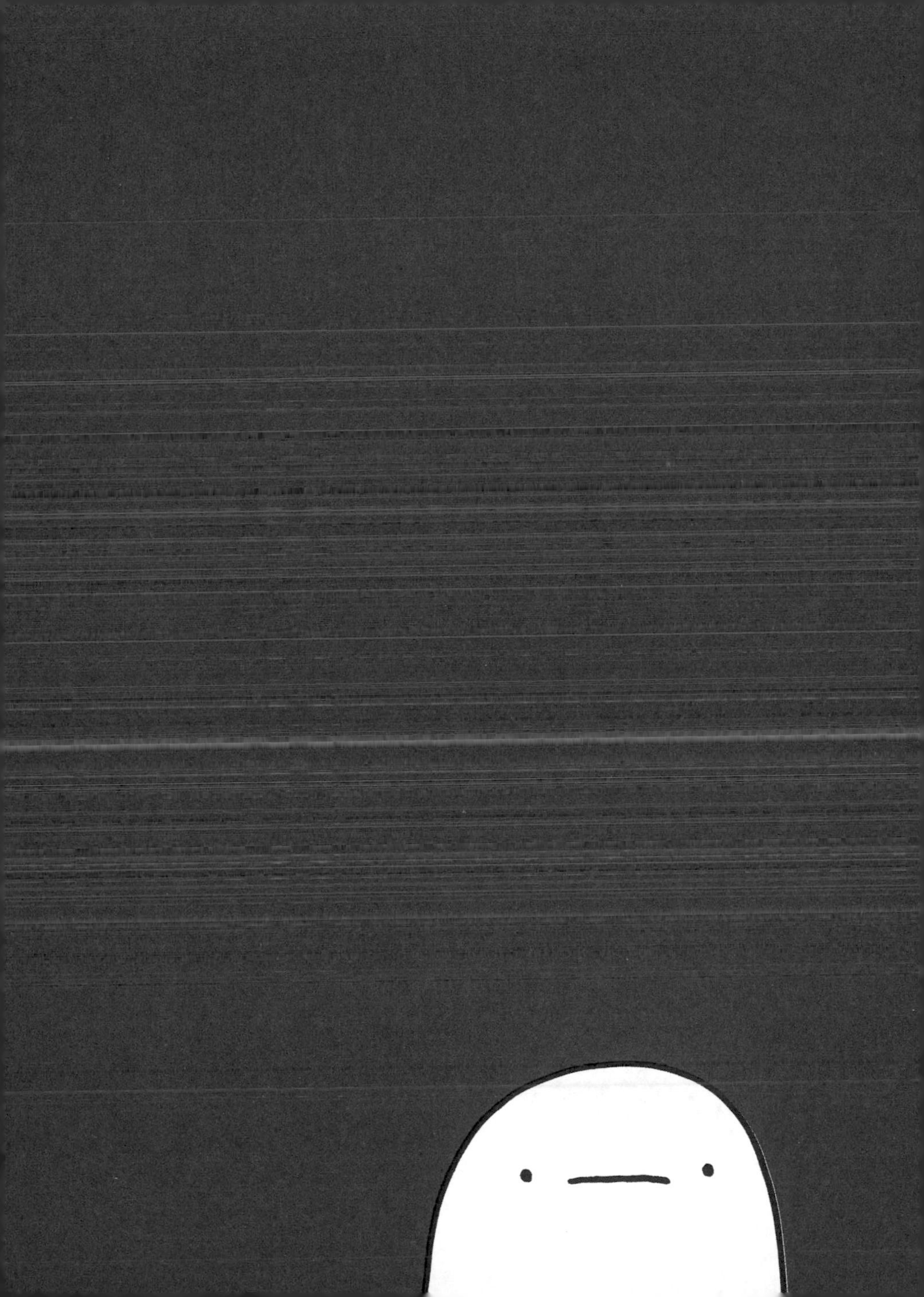

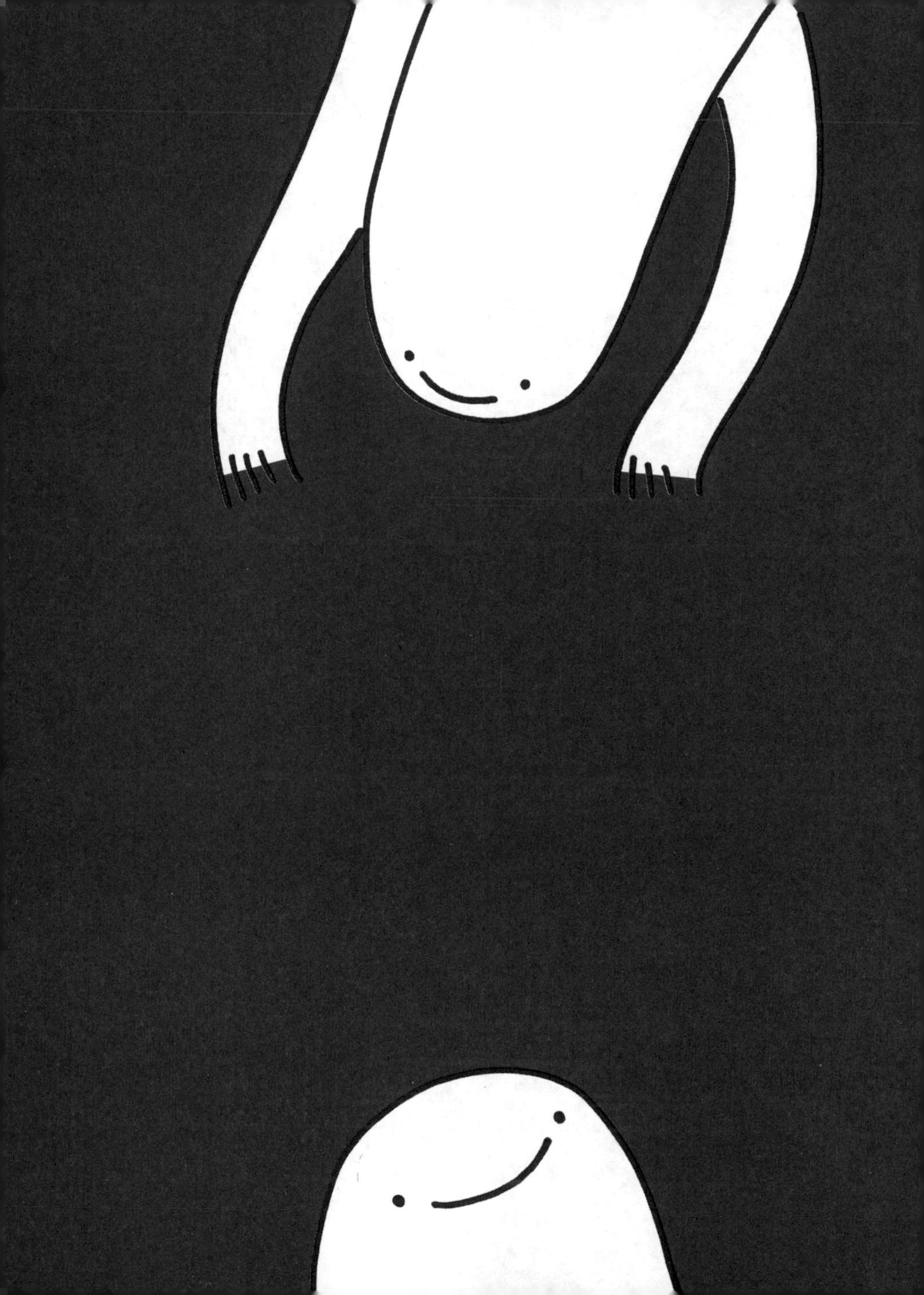

Hi, I'm Beth.

Welcome to the book and stuff!

Hey there,

Thanks for picking up this book. By doing so you are now on track to completely transform your life! . . . I'm kidding—oh my god, would that be annoying. Also, I'm a complete mess and not really in any position to tell people how to run their lives.

Maybe you're a little bit like me. Adulthood is exhausting and challenging, and you're still trying to find your place in this big wacky world, while everyone you used to know from school is getting married and posting about it online like the smug, successful people they are. So fun.

Maybe you've also felt sad and anxious, like *This depression is never-ending and I'm upset for no reason and sometimes television is the only thing that makes sense.* That's all right, and I've definitely been there. You're not alone in feeling that way.

I may not have the answers to your problems, life-changing tips, or really any idea what I'm doing, but I do have experience in making a half-assed attempt at adulthood. I also have a bunch of embarrassing stories, because embarrassment is one of the things I seem to be really good at. And there's some stuff on depression, anxiety, and legally being an adult but not really feeling like one.

Basically, what I'm trying to say is that you're okay. And sometimes just being okay is a great place to be.

Okay?

Things aren't always perfect,
but I'm here.

I'm better.

I'm me.

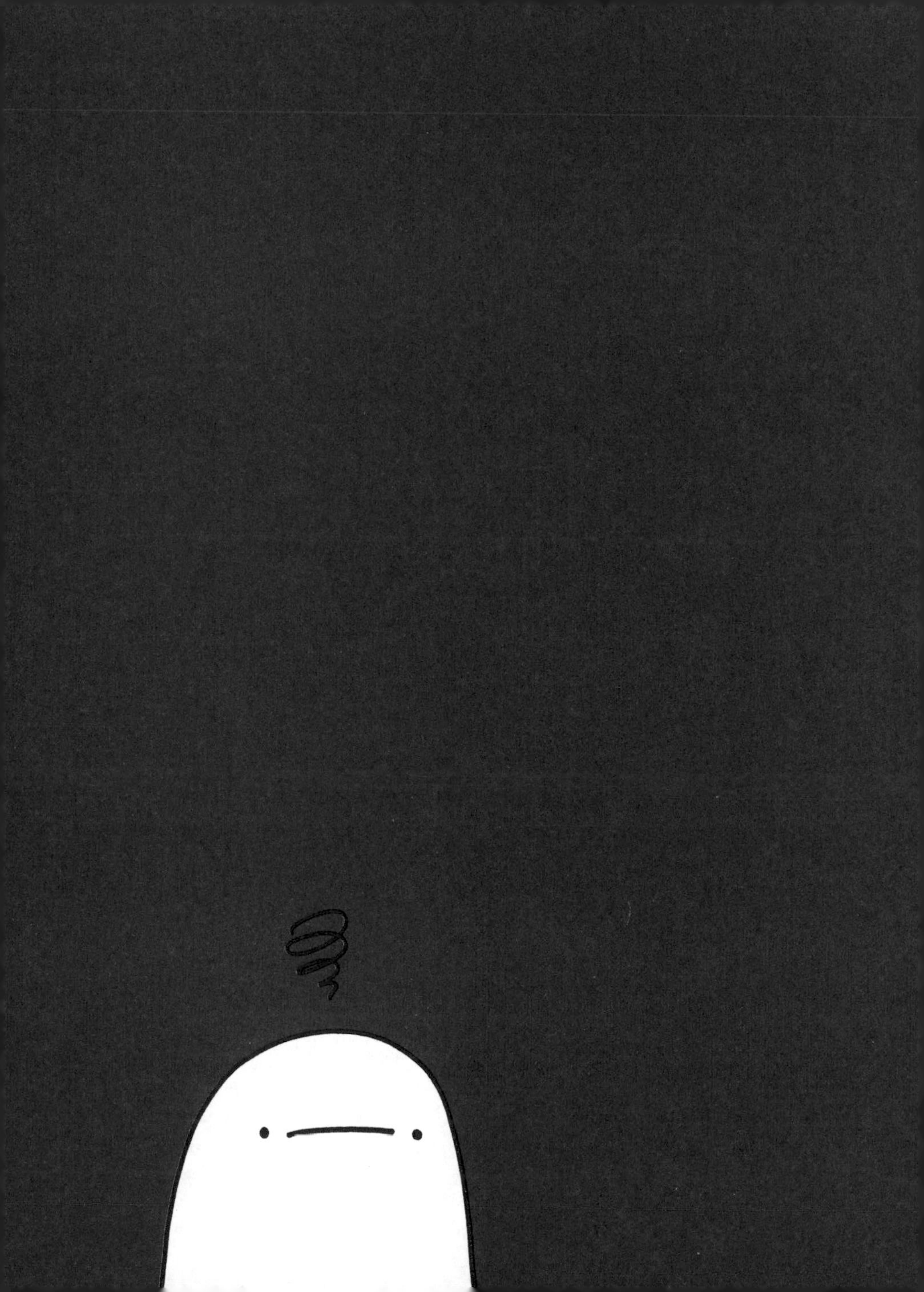

There is a special area of hell called LinkedIn. This website exists for the twisted purpose of letting you look up people you went to school with so you can frantically compare yourself with them. It is particularly helpful to those of us

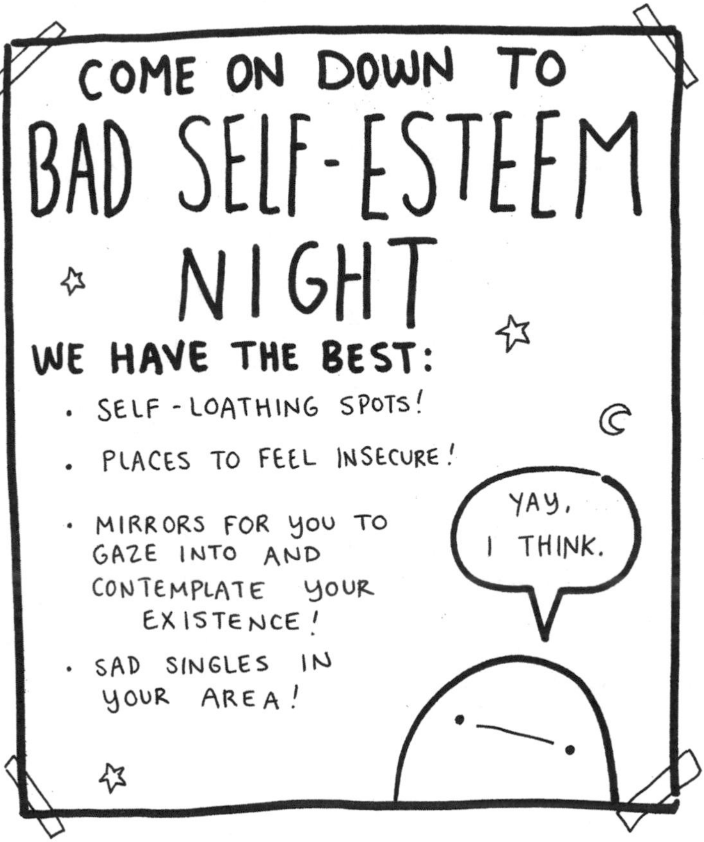
COME ON DOWN TO
BAD SELF-ESTEEM NIGHT
WE HAVE THE BEST:
• SELF-LOATHING SPOTS!
• PLACES TO FEEL INSECURE!
• MIRRORS FOR YOU TO GAZE INTO AND CONTEMPLATE YOUR EXISTENCE!
• SAD SINGLES IN YOUR AREA!
YAY, I THINK.

who are having a bad self-esteem night and need to be reminded just how not up to par we really are.

Viewing all the fancy places classmates are working and who their interesting connections are serves to remind us of how little we've accomplished. LinkedIn has probably made millions from my misery.

Comparing ourselves to other people is just a natural part of life. I do it in every way possible. Not because I'm looking to be better than anyone, but because *I'm that insecure*.

It can be minor things, like checking out how everyone else at a party is dressed to make sure you look okay, or major things, like getting really upset that the girl who was mean to you in school landed a prestigious job. And it can suck a lot when you feel you aren't as good, because getting out of that mind-set requires you to appreciate all the things you've done so far! Which, sometimes, is not as much as you would have liked.

I've wasted hours scrolling through the internet, peering at people's profiles and seeing how grown-up looking their pictures are. Medical students, teachers, law students—really, these people have accomplished a lot. And, oh god—*some of them are married, with families*. The nagging sense of competition begins, and I start to feel like I don't stack up in any way.

DAILY INSECURITIES

MY FACE

WHATEVER IS GOING ON IN MY EMAIL

THE CLOTHES I AM WEARING

HOW I COME ACROSS TO PEOPLE

SOMETHING ONLINE, PROBABLY

MY FACE (AGAIN)

"WAS I NICE ENOUGH OR AM I NEVER NICE ENOUGH?!?"

JOB LIFE CAREER FUTURE ETC.

... AND MY FACE (YET AGAIN)

THE SPIRAL OF LOOKING UP PEOPLE YOU USED TO KNOW

It can be hard enough to see the progress you've made in life, even without the distraction of an internet browser. Sometimes I really have to talk myself down—"Okay, they've got a stellar career and a million friends, but hey, I didn't cry in public today." The measure of progress is unique to each of us. Did it make you feel pretty good to achieve something, even if it was a tiny something? Hey, that's progress! And that's great!

HOW I SEE OTHER PEOPLE'S PROGRESS

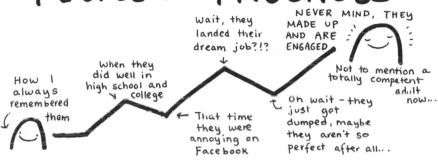

How I
always
remembered
them

When they
did well in
high school and
college

Wait, they
landed their
dream job?!?

← That time
they were
annoying on
Facebook

NEVER MIND, THEY
MADE UP
AND ARE
ENGAGED

Oh wait — they
just got
dumped, maybe
they aren't so
perfect after all...

Not to mention a
totally competent
adult
now...

HOW I SEE MY PROGRESS

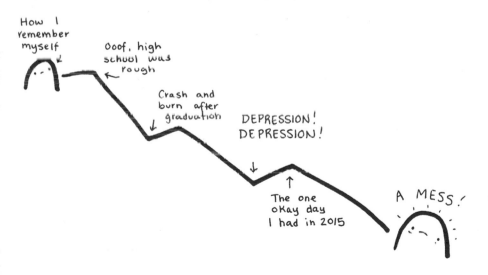

How I
remember
myself

Ooof, high
school was
rough

Crash and
burn after
graduation

DEPRESSION!
DEPRESSION!

The one
okay day
I had in 2015

A MESS!

A CONVERSATION
WITH MOM

Mom, I'm worried like
all the time, especially
before bed and when
I wake
up.

because all I can think about is WORK
WORK WORK and if I'm doing enough, and
like right now work occupies all my thoughts
and I just can't stop thinking about what

I need to do
next and what
could have
been done
better.

Am I okay?!?
Is there something
wrong with me?!?

I think it's just
called being an adult.

Well,
fuck.

There's always going to be someone out there who is doing better than you. There's also someone doing worse than you. It's an endless cycle of competition that's so unnecessary. And sometimes an old acquaintance will be putting it on Facebook. But the good news is that you get to create your own definition of progress and success. Maybe it's that you went to a doctor's appointment or convinced yourself not to look up so-and so online. Either way, a step forward is good, a step backward isn't the end of the world, and keeping both feet on the ground is great—sometimes that's actual progress. You've got this, no matter what your mom's friend says about her own kids. Because you're you, and really, there's no better success than that.

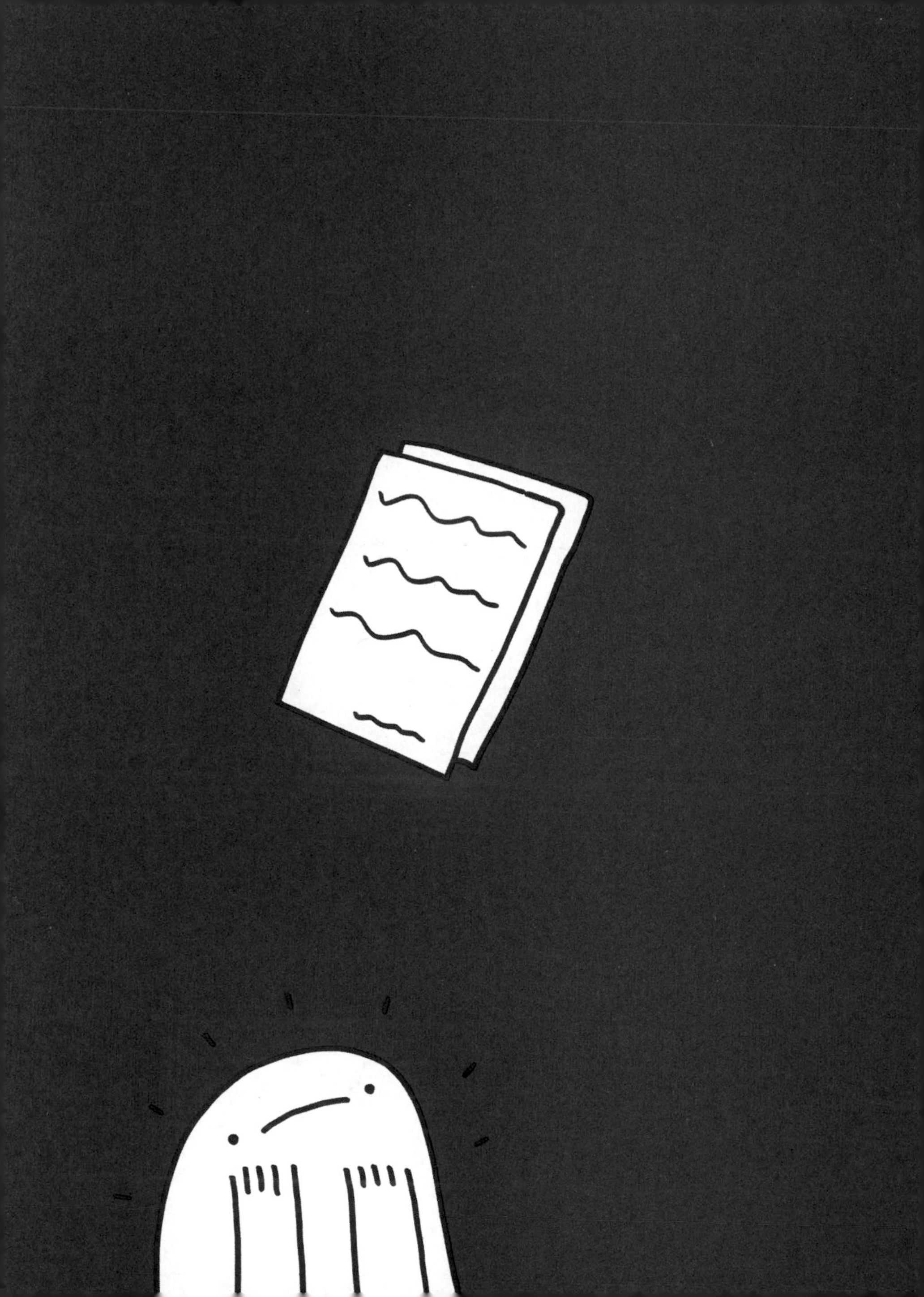

2

Sometimes I wonder if I am ever going to be ready for adult-hood, despite the fact that I am in my midtwenties. At first the whole thing seems like a glittering mirage: Freedom! Making my own choices! Being an adult should be a fun and exhilarating experience, but there is a boring side to it that often weighs me down. This mundane part includes taxes, bills, cleaning, and, worst of all, making any sort of phone call under any circumstance.

Making a phone call to the doctor is the worst kind of call you can possibly make. It's bad enough that you have to talk to another person on the phone, where you can't see their reaction, but you also have to discuss PERSONAL MEDICAL INFORMATION! How can one task hold the potential for so many disasters.

I had to make a phone call to the doctor's once, asking for an appointment for a personal problem. The problem being that I'm a cyclist, and I hurt my crotch from all the riding.

"Hello?" said the voice on the other end. I was nervous— *hello*, personal problems AND communication, eek!—and I said, "Hi, um, I'd like to make an appointment with my doctor. I'm a cyclist and my crotch really hurts from riding and I don't know if that's normal and anyway could I make that appointment?"

Silence.

"You have the wrong number. This is a different office."

Because being an adult doesn't automatically make you successful at interacting with other adults, especially when you're brand-new at it. In fact, a lot of us are really, really bad at

HOW TO DO LAUNDRY
LIKE AN ADULT

Put it all
in a basket.

Put it in the washer.

Put it in the dryer.

Shove it all back in
the basket.
You did laundry like
an adult!

Goodbye phone, you gotta go.

I'm your phone,

also known as a disaster waiting to happen!

PHONE CALLS
AS AN ADULT

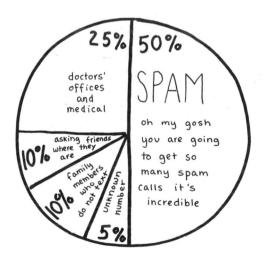

25% — doctors' offices and medical

50% SPAM

oh my gosh you are going to get so many spam calls it's incredible

10% — asking friends where they are

10% — family members who do not text

5% — unknown number

it. Because there is no officially sanctioned training guide or seminar, figuring out how to be an adult is done through trial and error. Yeah, it's embarrassing; yeah, you'll make bad conversation, but you're never alone in doing so. We've all done and said things we regret with a vengeance, and then wished the earth would swallow us up whole.

There have been other times that have really driven home my "adult" status. One New Year's Eve, everyone was back from college, and we were spending the night at my friend Brittany's house—it was great seeing her family again.

The night seemed to speed along, and before we knew it, midnight had struck, cheers were shouted, and another year had been rung in. Sleepily, we headed to bed on the couches in Brittany's basement.

When morning came, we were groggy from the night before. I was awake but kind of stared at the ceiling a bit, as it's always awkward being the first one up at these things. Then Krystal rolled over and shouted, "OH NO!"

The rest of us jolted up and looked at her.

"The floor! LOOK AT THE FLOOR!"

On the floor was the longest, blackest, scariest centipede we had ever seen. The legs all seemed to blur together as it scuttled along the carpet.

LET'S MEET THOSE INVOLVED...

BETH
me

ELI
my best friend since high school and general partner in crime

BRITTANY
my go-to for bad movies and all things pop culture

KRYSTAL
animation enthusiast with a wicked sense of humor

"What do we do?"

"It's too big to just squash!"

The four of us were paralyzed. Brittany jumped off the couch.

"DAD!" she shouted. "THERE'S A GIANT CENTIPEDE IN THE BASEMENT!"

There was a pause, and then a clinking noise.

Rolling along the bottom of the stairs was a can of bug spray. From upstairs, her dad called down, "You're old enough to get rid of it yourself!"

MUTUALLY ASSURED DESTRUCTION

BIG SCARY TAX FORM

PUT SOME
NUMBERS HERE,
NUMBERS ARE
REALLY GOOD!

NAME   CITY   STATE

GO ON!

ADDRESS   COUNTRY

PICK SOME!

WHAT YOUR DREAM WAS BEFORE ADULTHOOD STARTED

IT'S TOTALLY
OFFICIAL-LOOKING!

STATUS

- ☐ MARRIED
- ☐ SINGLE
- ☐ I'M NOT REALLY SURE WHAT IT IS YET
- ☐ LONELY

- ☐ PLAYING THE FIELD
- ☐ MARRIED TO A CELEBRITY IN MY MIND
- ☐ LOVE IS DEAD
- ☐ I LIKE CHECKING BOXES!

- ☐ CHECK THIS
- ☐ AND THIS
- ☐ ... ONLY IF YOU READ PAGE A4
- ☐ ... OH CRAP

EXEMPTIONS
LIST DEPENDENTS, LIKE CHILDREN!

_____

_____

_____

LIST IMAGINARY CHILDREN FROM YOUR IMAGINARY CELEBRITY MARRIAGE

_____

_____

_____

ARE YOU SICK OF ALL THESE QUESTIONS ABOUT KIDS WHEN YOU CAN BARELY TAKE CARE OF YOURSELF?

- ☐ YES
- ☐ OH YES

INCOME

1   GET READY, IT'S GONNA GET COMPLICATED

1A   SERIOUSLY

2   UH... I KNOW I MAKE MONEY AND STUFF

3   I AM BEING PUNISHED WITH FORMS I DON'T UNDERSTAND

4   I NEED A REAL ADULT

SWIPING YOUR CARD

WHAT (NORMALLY) HAPPENS

SWIPE NOW	AUTHORIZING...	APPROVED! THANKS!

WHAT IT FEELS LIKE

SWIPE NOW	HEY, IT'S DEBIT, DO YOU HAVE ENOUGH IN YOUR ACCOUNT?	NO, REALLY, PLEASE MENTALLY GO OVER EVERY PURCHASE YOU MADE THIS WEEK
IF YOU ARE DECLINED, YOU'RE GOING TO HAVE TO EXPLAIN YOURSELF TO THE CASHIER, WON'T THAT BE FUN?!?	AUTHORIZING...	APPROVED! (THIS TIME, ANYWAY)

In that moment we became four adults—four adults who did not know how to kill a giant centipede. So we huddled together behind one couch, staring at it. And we knew we couldn't get rid of the centipede, so we settled on leaving it alone if it left us alone. Because sometimes adult things are too scary, and you just deal with it the best you can.

Some things just take time. Figuring out banking stuff, how to make budgets, disposing of bugs, and calling people for help takes repeated trial and error.

I can't count the number of times my card has been declined because I didn't budget or know the exact amount in my bank account.

The error portion is a part of being an adult, although we often see adulthood as something that other people are just very good at, that no one ever messes up. The reality is more like this: mistakes are made, and making them is how we learn to avoid those same mistakes in the future.

Maybe being more adult-like means checking your bank statements or learning to listen to the whole information menu on the phone before telling a stranger about your crotch problems. We've all been there. It's okay.

You're okay. You've got this.

Don't buy things! Be responsible and save your money!

but it's on sale

We're getting it.

That's such a good price!

We're totally getting it.

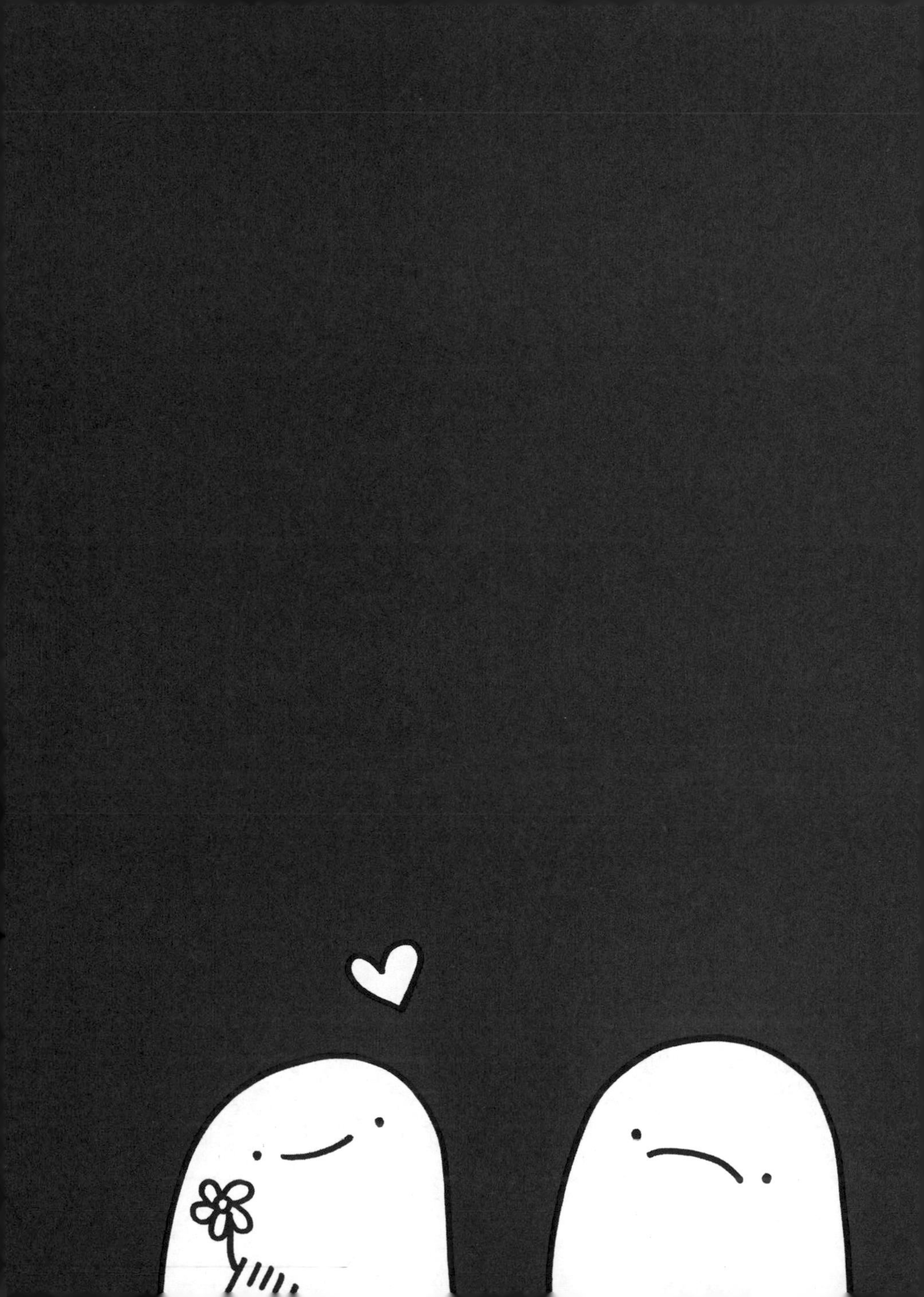

I think figuring out how to befriend people is hard. It's even harder to figure out how to date people. It's like, *Great, I have to do all the stuff you expect from a friend AND have you*

be the romantic focus of my life? Do you even know how much time that eats up?

Celebrity crushes can be a good outlet for a while, but they can also lead to loneliness.

THE CELEBRITY CRUSH CYCLE

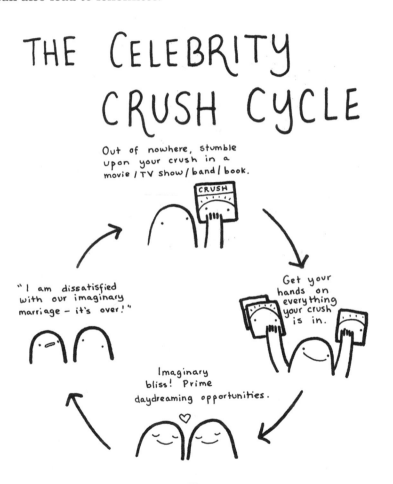

Out of nowhere, stumble upon your crush in a movie / TV show / band / book.

Get your hands on everything your crush is in.

Imaginary bliss! Prime daydreaming opportunities.

"I am dissatisfied with our imaginary marriage – it's over!"

THE HUMAN CRUSH CYCLE

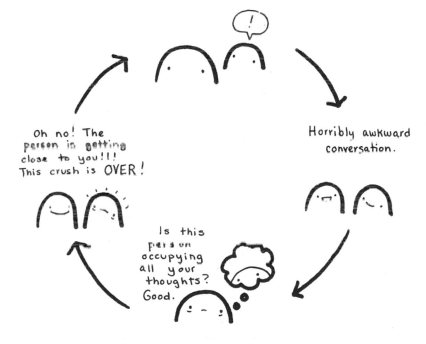

Find someone interesting.

Horribly awkward conversation.

Is this person occupying all your thoughts? Good.

Oh no! The person is getting close to you!!! This crush is OVER!

Then, of course, there's the super fun stage of dating when you don't know what you are.

Not to mention how difficult it is to even get to that point. First impressions can be complete chaos.

IS IT A DATE?

Sometimes it can be hard to tell if you're actually on a date or just hanging out. This guide can help you decide!

Wanna get together sometime?

VERDICT: ????

I'm having a really nice time with you!

VERDICT: who knows.

Here, let me pay.

VERDICT: Maybe?!?

I'm totally not setting you two up! This is just because I think you can talk about a lot!

VERDICT: Oh yes, this is a date.

I went on a disastrous date a few years ago that really exemplified the pitfalls of awkward early dating. I had met the guy through friends of friends, and we exchanged numbers, agreeing to go out. When the night came, we met at a casual restaurant, but I was too nervous to eat anything. I didn't really know what to say—one on-one conversations can be enough pressure even without the premise of a date. As it turned out, this was okay because my date had plenty to say about literally everything.

He was very into himself and was full of opinions. We just didn't click. If he said "day," I said "night" . . . at least, I would have if he had left me any room to talk. But I didn't know the proper way to end the evening without being rude, so I sat there in a horribly awkward manner making vague agreeing sounds at whatever he was saying. Finally it seemed like things were wrapping up and I would soon be able to return to the magical land called home. Then, just as my freedom was in reach, he spoke words that crushed my world:

"Hey, can I get a ride?"

For the record, you don't owe anyone a ride, even if you went on a date with them. But because I was young and startled, I said, "Sure." In my mind, it was a step toward getting out of the restaurant and closer to home. We walked to my car and

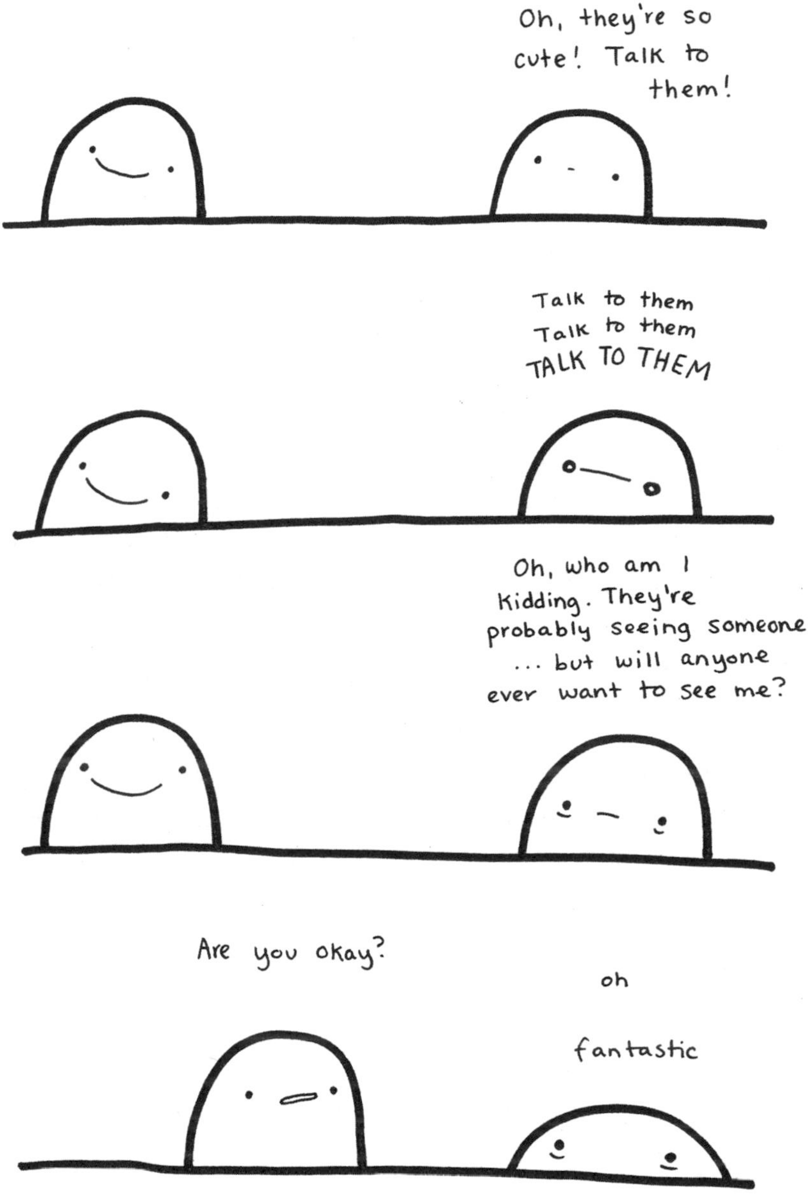
Oh, they're so cute! Talk to them!
Talk to them
Talk to them
TALK TO THEM
Oh, who am I kidding. They're probably seeing someone ... but will anyone ever want to see me?
Are you okay?
oh
fantastic

drove mostly in silence, until he suggested I put on some music. Now, I had spent the better part of the evening listening to his opinions on music. I had been told what the pinnacle of good music was (punk) and what shouldn't be listened to (not punk). Without hesitating, I told him to pull the CD out of the door on his side and pop it in.

As soon as the opening synthesizer notes of "Tom Sawyer" began, he was trapped in progressive-rock hell until we reached his house. I was using Rush's seminal 1981 album *Moving Pictures* as punishment, because I knew he would find it so uncool. The journey was agonizing for both of us—me, because I was in close proximity to someone who I was obvi-

ously not getting along with, and him, well . . . the look on his face said it all. Every foot we drove felt like a mile. When he got out of the car, I felt relief—I could see the light at the end of the tunnel. Then he turned to me and said, "Hey, wanna come inside?"

Oh god, my prog-rock defense shield hadn't worked. *He was still interested.* This was a dire situation that called for a dire solution. I turned the music up—track two, "Red Barchetta"—as loud as it could go and started shouting, "WHAT? I CAN'T HEAR YOU!" gesturing wildly to indicate this. "I DON'T KNOW WHAT YOU'RE SAYING. I HAVE TO GO NOW, GOODBYE!" I waved manically, and the pitch of my shrieking was pretty much in sync with Geddy Lee's at this point. I awkwardly leaned over and did my best to slam the door shut as fast as I could.

He stood bewildered in the driveway. I pulled away and did not look back, letting the thundering opening of "YYZ" take me home.

Love is hard enough without all the pressures of good first impressions and potentially having to torture your date with progressive rock. It's also a matter of seeing yourself as worthy of love and accepting all the different sides you have. It's a bit like a diamond, where all the intricate dimensions and sparkly bits make up one really great whole. Seeing those pieces come together to make someone complete is what love is all about. And being able to see that in yourself can be the hardest thing of all.

Self-love is all over the place right now, as a positive movement to help people accept themselves. But for a lot of us, it can be a real challenge. I often wonder things like, *How can I, a complete and total garbage can of awfulness, find it in the trash that is me to love not only myself, but other people?* It's a tall order for anyone, especially for someone with low self-esteem.

SELF-LOVE
IS HARD

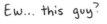

Ew... this guy?

Uh. Same, buddy.

For me, it's often just picking one little piece of my trash that I really do like. It's never something broad and grand, like *I am so pretty today; I hope everyone sees how pretty I am!* It's often a small and insignificant detail, like *I picked out a nice shade of nail polish* or *I have really great taste in music that no one, especially not my dates, ever appreciates.* It's the little things we like about ourselves that often make the other pieces fall in line and click together, forming a nice whole. Self-love is going to be impossible some days and can seem like the most daunting challenge ever. After all, we allow ourselves to get frustrated and annoyed with others, so it's only natural to feel that way about ourselves sometimes. We are with ourselves 24/7, and that's a lot of freaking time to spend with someone.

Be nice, be kind, be gentle with yourself and others. Wear nice nail polish, listen to the music you like, and the rest will come together. Or something.

Our brains aren't always the most reliable allies, and yet they get to call the shots on how we live our daily lives.

The stress they can bring is enormous, and sometimes it feels like an endless battle just to make it through the day. Also, I think my brain hates me.

It's a little weird to think of a major organ having a vendetta against you, but I honestly believe it. No other body part has consistently given me this much trouble while at the same time making me feel like the most worthless person on the planet.

For those unfamiliar with anxiety attacks, it's kind of like being shoved off a ledge without being able to scream. It's a silent takeover during which your body decides what's going to happen, and all logic is tossed aside. What makes it even more challenging is that it sometimes happens in public. Then, not only do you have to figure out how to take care of yourself, but you have to try not to alarm those around you, too.

Take, for example, the time my friends and I went to see Dylan Moran do a stand-up show in Chicago. Going out to events always makes me panic, no matter how much I want to have a good time. The situation was unbelievably frustrating. I was with people I liked, I was going to see a performer I liked, and all I could think about was running far, far away. I spent most of dinner shaking and crying in my seat, desperate to hide it from everyone around me, and I was sure they were all staring. What should have been a happy and fun experience ended with me heaving over a diner toilet due to my anxiety. I began to relax a bit only when the show started. And even though I was laughing along with the jokes, I still had lingering fear eating away at my stomach.

Anxiety is a powerful thing, and when it decides to strike, it can take many different, often demoralizing forms. Suddenly the only thing you can focus on is the absolute, fundamental sense of dread and upset storming inside you. When I'm anxious, I become absolutely obsessed with keeping everyone around me calm. It's almost like the minute I start to feel bad, I need to focus on someone else instead of on what's happening to me.

Another fun thing that goes along with my anxiety is obsessive-compulsive disorder. It's a condition based on intrusive thoughts and rituals—unwelcome thoughts come in, and in reaction you perform a ritual to counteract them. There's this belief that obsessive-compulsive disorder is a charming and quirky thing to have—hey, you like things alphabetical and color coded! It's regularly the butt of jokes, there are OCD-branded prank products available, and it's frequently considered an adorable character trait in TV shows, films, and books.

What most people don't see is the absolute misery and pain that go along with it.

Here's the thing about anxiety and planning to do stuff:

When you make plans and cancel, people sometimes get upset,

which is the last thing I want!

It's like, "yes! I want to do the activity! Very. very badly, too!"

But my panic takes over, not just mentally. but physically.

My chest hurts, and worse, my stomach rolls and gets nauseous, and I throw up.

! !!!

So I end up canceling,

which lets down not only other people,

but myself.

So now I have all this guilt and self-loathing,

not to mention the eternal " I AM MISSING OUT ON SO MUCH " feeling,

and sometimes it can be Too Much.

It's okay to take a few steps back and acknowledge that not everything is going to be easy for everyone — we all have strengths and weaknesses,

and just because something isn't a possibility now, doesn't mean it won't be in the future.

ACTIVITY

We all feel scared of doing stuff, even if it's something we want to do,

and canceling plans isn't the end of the world (even if it feels that way).

You can cancel plans, but you can't cancel how great you are !

I've dealt with obsessive-compulsive disorder from a young age. Things really began to go haywire around second grade. We had begun learning about illness in school, and I became absolutely fixated on germs. Suddenly everything seemed contaminated. I would wrap myself up at night in multiple blankets, cocooning myself against germs that could definitely get me, and I would lie awake for hours and hours, worrying. If you look back at my journals from the time, I wrote literally page after page about contamination.

Soon my fears really began to impact my life. I didn't like shaking hands with people or hugging other kids, and I always worried that some unknown virus would get me. My brain adjusted to this by giving me various tasks to complete. *Turn the light switch on and off before bed. Wash your hands four times. Step in and out of the doorway twice. Do these and you will be safe. Everyone will be safe.*

As I got older and more stressed out, the obsessive-compulsive disorder really turned up a notch. Public bathrooms became a nightmare, school dances were a misery (dancing *and* touching people!), and my tasks began to spiral out of control. Sometimes I would stand at the light switch flicking it on and off fifty or more times until it felt right. People began to notice my habits, and I would try to shrug them off as weird things

When I was younger, I had a hard time managing my OCD, because I didn't know what it was — just that I had to do things in order to feel okay.

But one day, I forgot to do any of my rituals or pay attention to my systems because it was Christmas, and I just wanted to have a nice time.

The next day, I saw the newspaper and totally freaked out.

NEWS

TSUNAMI STRIKES AND KILLS THOUSANDS

I didn't do my rituals + something bad happened =

IT'S ALL MY FAULT

This is my fault...

You see, OCD is a bit of a cycle for me:

FEAR

"Okay, but nothing is wrong now, sooo... "

Ritual brings comfort

Feeling okay

And since I broke that cycle for a day, and a disaster happened, I really internalized it as

My Fault.

Logically, as an adult I now know that I did not cause a disaster by not flipping a light switch five times, but that's the thing about OCD! It lets you think you did!

As I've gotten older, my OCD cycle has changed a bit:

FEAR ↘

Ritual brings comfort

↓

"Wait, do I really need to be doing this? Really?!?"

"I'm outta here, bye!" ←

Nope, not today.

I'm able to handle the impulses to do rituals a lot better, although I still struggle with it at times.

Sometimes I have to be patient with myself, and realize that while I can't kick OCD to the curb all the time, I can have good days...

... and the more good days I have, the better I feel.

I did. It's not like I wanted to be doing these tasks—my brain just said I had to if I wanted to be okay. As long as I kept cool about it, maybe people around me would, too.

It wasn't until I started therapy as an adult that I realized this was a mental health issue and that there were steps I could take to address it. And while some of the tasks got easier to manage as I worked harder to distract myself, I started to get really, really sad about the stigma associated with OCD. People treated obsessive-compulsive disorder as a fun character trait but were totally ignorant of the sheer anxiety that went along with it. While others were having a good laugh over straightening books (*That's soooo OCD!*), they never really saw the gripping panic of not being able to close the door "correctly," or the massive crying fit caused by not cleaning the bathroom "right" at two A.M.

Things really came to a breaking point for me at my friend's birthday party one year. A group of us went to a restaurant for a good night out. Toward the end of the dinner, several of us had to use the bathroom, so we all went together. I had worked especially hard over the past few years to be able to even use a public bathroom, and I thought this wouldn't be a big deal. The line was a bit long, but we had plenty to chat about, which helped distract me from some of my fears.

WHAT PEOPLE THINK MY OCD IS LIKE

Haha, I'm so organized!

Oooh, a little bit of dirt, better get that! Cleaning! Love it!

Oooh, I love color-coding AND organizing!

WHAT MY OCD IS LIKE

I have so many systems and rules to follow that I am a mess.

WELL, it's all contaminated and now I gotta do it all again with  my weird-ass rules and I hate this.

Who are you?!? Not me, that's for sure.

Finally my turn to use the toilet came, and I walked into a stall . . . only to find myself starting to panic. My stomach lurched, my chest tightened, and I began to freak out. Sometimes old fears are hard to let go of. I walked out of that stall and into the next available one, hoping that it would be clean enough to meet whatever ridiculous standards my brain had set this time.

And then I heard them talking.

This woman—literally right outside my stall—started going on about "I don't understand, she just walked into that stall and walked out?" "Oh, it looked fine to me. I wonder what her problem is?" *And then they started laughing.* I sat on that toilet and silently cried, because in that moment all the effort I had made seemed to be for nothing. What was the point of trying to get better if complete strangers—grown women—were just going to treat me like a joke? I refused to come out until I was sure they had left the bathroom.

Anxiety is hard enough to deal with on your own and even harder to want to tackle when people make fun of you. Finding balance is truly a daily struggle. Sometimes keeping your head up seems impossible, especially when it's easier to just give in to fear, even though you know it's not good for you. But each little step toward conquering those fears is good, and a

LET'S GO OUT!

It can be hard putting yourself back out there and doing things again — and yes, it might not be totally perfect,

so here is a quick guide to small activities that can gradually build into bigger and more fun ones!

INTRODUCTORY LEVEL

GROCERY STORE
BIG BOX RETAIL
POST OFFICE
CASUAL EATERY

All of these places are great because you don't have to commit to them — you can leave at any time, and there are exits you can see. There's also limited human interaction, so don't worry if you are scared of messing up!

EASY LEVEL

SHOPPING MALL
OUTDOOR PARK
SMALL SHOP
SIT-DOWN EATERY

These places build on the ones from above, and can be a bit more challenging, as they take commitment and invite conversation. You're more likely to be approached at places like malls, tiny shops, or parks, and it's okay if you don't know what to say; we all screw that up!

MEDIUM LEVEL

MOVIE THEATER
OUT WITH FRIENDS
VISITING FAMILY
MUSEUM / TOUR

The training wheels are off — these places all involve some level of commitment but still offer an exit strategy. They're great for practice if there's a big scary thing you really want to do! Put your coping skills to use here and don't be afraid to try — you got this!

HARD LEVEL

DAY TRIP
CONCERT / SHOW
DINNER PARTY
MAJOR LIFE EVENT

These can be a challenge but very rewarding! They require a longer period of commitment and they're hard to run away from. Social interaction is a must. If things go wrong, it can feel like you never want to try again, but trying and trying is key here. Make sure you have an anxiety plan in place, and you know what to do!

It might seem scary, but you can totally do this!

Anxiety sucks, but you can be prepared.

No matter how bad it is, you can totally do this!

ANXIETY PLAN

WHAT KIND OF ANXIETY ARE YOU HAVING?

☐ SPECIFIC - I know exactly what is wrong

☐ GENERAL- I have no idea why I am feeling this way

⫶ GENERAL ⫶

Sometimes your body decides to feel awful NOW. It's crummy and general anxiety can be very upsetting.

You can try to pinpoint the cause by seeing if your current panic is similar to any past panics you may have had.

⫶ DO SOMETHING ⫶

Anxiety thrives on taking control so it's your entire focus. Trying something — anything — to combat it is good!

⫶ SPECIFIC ⫶

If you know what's wrong and why you feel upset, take a look at the problem — is there anything you can actively change?

If not, imagine a bit about what you wish would happen instead.

And remember — battling an anxiety monster can be too much for one person.

Don't be afraid to ask for help!

YOUR ANXIETY PLAN

A KINDA FUN FILL-IN LIST

The kind of anxiety I am feeling is...

☐ SPECIFIC
☐ GENERAL

List some stuff that's been going on lately ↓

_____
_____
_____
_____

CALM DOWN

Here are some calm-down, chill-out ideas if you're having a hard time :

☐ take a walk ☐ text someone
☐ listen to music ☐ pet a dog
☐ watch a video you like
☐ wash your face ☐ hydrate!
☐ slow your breathing down
☐ brush your teeth ☐ do a mindless chore
☐ write down your feelings
☐ rip up your written feelings
☐ ignore the internet / email
☐ smell something strong (like perfume!)
☐ gently stretch
☐ touch different surfaces and focus on the textures

B O N U S !

CALM DOWN: "STUCK IN PUBLIC" EDITION

☐ move your fingers in a comforting rhythm
☐ find a wall and lean against it
☐ take yourself out of the crowd
☐ focus on your breathing / heart rate
☐ doodle or write nonsense
☐ change your body posture
☐ splash cold water on your face

step backward doesn't mean all your work was for nothing. I prefer to think of each thing that happened to me as an "experience." Yes, what happened at the restaurant was a bad experience, but it still counts in the overall "experience" category, and the more I do things, the more I learn. The important thing with anxiety is to not let it stop you from doing things ever again. For a long time I flat-out refused to go to concerts or stand-up gigs. But that just made me upset in a different way, because I was missing out. And I've grown quite a bit in how I handle my anxiety now; I actually show up and deal with it. I've had successful nights out to see performances, and I've used public bathrooms plenty of times since without incident. Those little steps, both good and bad, are so important when it comes to managing anxiety.

I went to a concert recently. It was my first big, real concert in a long time—many years, in fact. And I was so nervous; I was nervous driving there, parking, finding my seat. What if I freaked out? Threw up? Cried? But as the night went on I kept having a better and better time. And when the actual concert started, I was cheering with everyone else. Midway through the performance, an important thought struck me:

I'm really glad I did this.

No matter how comfortable you are with feelings, it can
be incredibly challenging learning to express them in a
healthy way.

I participated in martial arts for a number of years when I was younger. At first it was a really fun after-school activity, and I enjoyed meeting new people, running around, and engaging in gentle sparring with my classmates. But then a new teacher took over, and everything changed.

He was fairly intense, someone you knew immediately not to mess with. Gone were the before-class giggles, replaced with quiet, tense moments waiting for the session to begin. Fortunately he didn't teach too many of the classes, and I still got to crack a few smiles with my regular instructors. In a sport that values technique and perfection, I often wasn't perfect, but I still had a good time working on improving. My teachers were patient and helped me when I freaked out, and I continued to advance through the courses.

By the time I reached the upper levels, this man was exclusively teaching the sessions. While other instructors were mindful of the students' limits and often took them into account during sparring, he would typically come at me full force, pulling no punches. He always stopped before anything got physically out of hand, but it was demotivating knowing a middle-aged man was going to hurl himself at me, and that he would win every time.

It was ten times more discouraging knowing he was going to make me cry.

If he didn't like giggling before class, he hated crying during class, and I always wound up crying during his classes. I would be working with a partner, struggling to get my coordination right, and he would get in my face about it. Normally when I began to look stressed my other instructors would give me a few seconds to calm down, remind me that I was doing okay, and then we'd try it again. He didn't do any of that; instead he would say, "Are you going to cry again?" and give me this look like I was causing all the trouble in the world. And I would start to cry, partially from being so worried about doing the moves correctly and partially because I was so scared that I might cry that I ended up crying.

"Well, if you're going to cry, you have to leave the room," he would say with an air of authority, and would proceed to dismiss me in front of all my classmates. It was humiliating, having to wait in the lobby with the parents. During this time I was probably supposed to be composing myself, but I was usually so embarrassed that I would endlessly unlace and relace my shoes, because at least it gave me something to do. Then, like clockwork, he would come out to the lobby, making a big show of it, and say, "If you think you've calmed down enough you can come back to class." This process repeated over and over again, with me freaking out, him egging me on, and me getting thrown out, until I finally just quit altogether.

Even though I spent years of my life working on perfecting my movements, coordination, and response times, my biggest takeaway from the experience was that showing any emotion was bad and I needed to be perfect. Not good—perfect. I mastered the skill of shoving down any emotions that were bothering me, and I worried a lot about anyone seeing me crying. Tears became a reason for shame, and achieving perfection became a burning desire in all aspects of my life.

WHAT A BAD DAY LOOKS LIKE

WHAT IT FEELS LIKE

BOTTLE IT UP

I'm fine.*

* I'm fine.

I'm fine.*

* Things could be better.

I'm fine.*

* I'm really not so great.

I'm fine.*

* I'm upset, actually.

I'm fine.*

* Yeah, I'm really upset.

I'm fine.*

* I'm upset, and I want to talk about it but I don't know how.

I'm fine.*

* It's eating away at me, and I'm really not fine.

I'm fine.*

* This is not good at all.

I'm not fine.*

* Great, so it had to come to this in order for me to express how I'm feeling?

EXPRESS IT!

Yes, expressing your feelings sucks, and it can be scary — but it can also be an emotional weight lifted off your shoulders.

 Here are some things I've learned:

"I" statements help, and the person you're talking to is more likely to understand where you're coming from — "you" statements can be off-putting.

If you can't quite pin an actual problem down, concentrate on the emotions you're feeling and work from there.

Sometimes communication goes badly and the other person might not understand what you mean or how you feel. Don't let it stop you from trying!

You've gotta be honest with yourself before you can share feelings with others.

I was obsessed with being perfect and burying any feeling that wasn't happiness. I was functioning, but I wasn't being me. I was presenting to the world a polished version of myself, where you couldn't see all the cracks and dents that were chipped away inside. It was an unhealthy way of being. Good or bad, nice or disgusting, feelings are feelings, and they exist whether you want them to or not.

You'll have to deal with them sooner or later, and bottling them up only leads to further distress. Owning your emotions definitely isn't an easy task, but it's an essential one. Feelings are there to let you know when something is wrong or to reassure you that you're on the right track. The sooner you choose to acknowledge them, the more relieved both you and your feelings will be.

6

SLEEP IS
JUST DEATH
WITHOUT THE
COMMITMENT

It was my high school graduation party, and it was supposed to be the happiest day of my school career. As I stood on my parents' back deck, watching everyone talking, laughing, and gossiping about the end of the year, I started to feel this sinking sensation in my stomach. *This is it? Is this as good as it gets? How did things go so wrong?*

I had been a good student throughout the years and was diligent about turning in all my work, studying for every test, and pushing myself to succeed academically. All I had ever dreamed of was becoming a nurse. From the time I was a kid, I took care of all my stuffed animals and their various ailments, dreaming of the day I could do it for real. While I wasn't top of the class and certainly had my struggles, I did okay in school and kept myself on the right track to achieving my goal.

In high school, things had started to falter. I began to struggle academically, falling behind in mathematics, and I had a hard time keeping up in even the remedial classes. I still wanted to be a nurse in the worst way, and I signed up for every medical-related class I could get into. I got a volunteer job at my local hospital, working in the gift shop and making deliveries. Every time I put on my volunteer jacket, it reminded me I was one step closer to the real thing. I pushed myself further and further academically, working on my math before school and during lunch. And then the best news came—I qualified for my high school's internship program at the hospital. I would get to spend two hours every day of my senior year following doctors and nurses and interacting with patients.

And then the first day of rotations came. I was in the oncology unit, shadowing a quiet doctor. I felt slightly out of place in the formal work clothes the high school interns wore, self-conscious of the *click-clack* my heels made in the hallway. We got to our first room, and the doctor dove right in. Chatting with the patient, removing her bandages, checking a wound for signs of infection—it was too much for me. My head began to spin. I excused myself, saying I was feeling a bit nauseated, which everyone understood.

In reality, I was scared. I was so, so scared. Because while the rest of my friends were enjoying their senior year of high school, sitting in study hall in their sweat pants, talking about dances, I was standing in a stiff dress and uncomfortable heels, chasing a career I thought I wanted and suddenly realized I didn't. It was too much of a commitment too soon.

But what we want isn't always what we need.

I dropped the internship the next day, much to the shock of my parents, teachers, guidance counselor, and friends. I lied and told everyone I couldn't handle the sight of blood, and that I wasn't sure nursing was a good match for me. In reality,

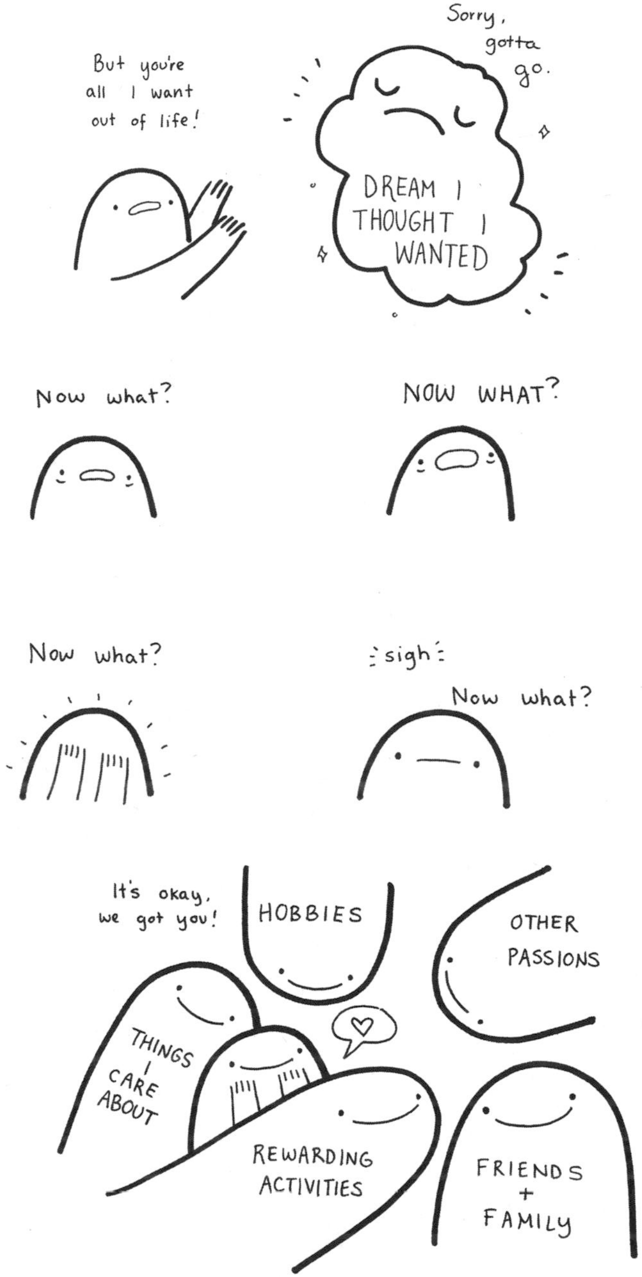
But you're all I want out of life!
Sorry, gotta go.
DREAM I THOUGHT I WANTED
Now what?
NOW WHAT?
Now what?
sigh
Now what?
It's okay, we got you!
HOBBIES
OTHER PASSIONS
THINGS I CARE ABOUT
REWARDING ACTIVITIES
FRIENDS + FAMILY

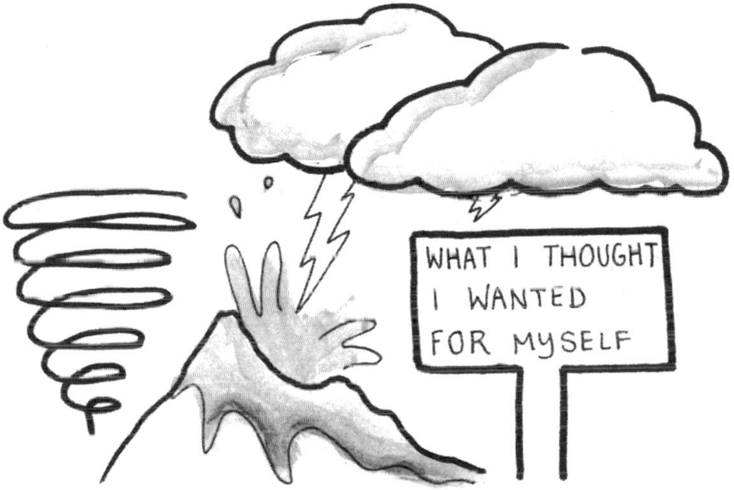
WHAT I THOUGHT I WANTED FOR MYSELF

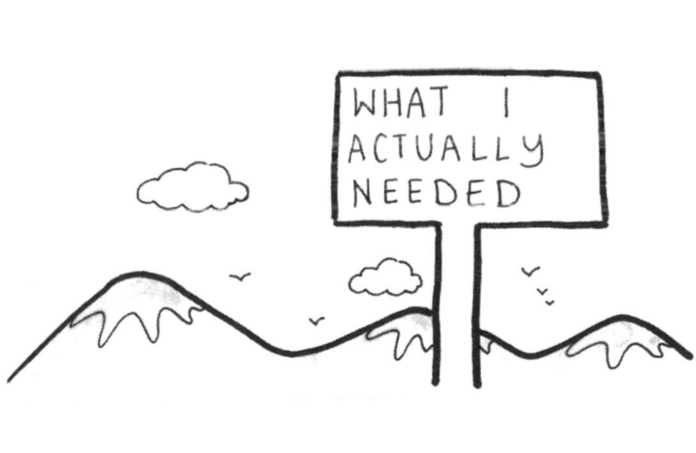
WHAT I ACTUALLY NEEDED

I was getting very frightened about the future. Graduation was looming, and everything I had trained and prepared for felt very upside down. I didn't know what to do, even with the most basic parts of my routine. I couldn't keep volunteering at the hospital, so I chose to quit. It was just a reminder of the future I had walked away from.

I began to flounder.

Without my goal and direction I lost motivation. I stopped turning in all my assignments, slacked off, and started ditching class. I stopped hanging out with my friends, reasoning that since they were leaving me to go away to school the following fall, I might as well leave them first. I was miserable and spent many nights locked in my closet, huddled among my clothes, wishing the back wall led to another world. School became enormously painful, because there was so much emphasis on celebrating that it was coming to an end. Everyone was eagerly anticipating their new changes, and I felt more stuck than ever before. I also slept every chance I could get. Something about being unconscious was comforting, like I could just turn my brain off for a while.

The big scary graduation day came, and as the sun was setting, everyone threw their caps into the air. As I watched the chaos unfold and the caps fly, I secretly looked up at the sky and wished it would suck me up.

Life after graduation was painful. My friends spent the summer packing up and picking out things for their dorm rooms, and I became more distant. I spent a lot of time in my room, and I couldn't stand to think about the future more than a few days ahead. Sleep began to occupy more and more time, which worried my parents—I had never been a big sleeper, and suddenly it was the only thing I wanted to do.

As the months marched on, my friends left for college across the country, and I enrolled in a local school. I continued to live at home with my family. The only change between high school and college was that I had more time to sleep between classes. I wasn't really trying to learn, and just getting up every day became agonizing. School wasn't a priority for me—what was the point of even working at it if I didn't know what I wanted? I hated all my classes and hated doing the work even more. I couldn't seem to make friends with anyone. My life was rapidly unraveling, and I began using an unhealthy coping mechanism to get through—self-injury.

Self harm was something that I occasionally used in high school to deal with my emotions. I couldn't really talk to anyone about how I was feeling, but I was into the idea of "punishing" myself for things I didn't do right. So I cut myself. I'd always kept it hidden and done it sparingly, but in college it became a more frequent occurrence.

One dark December night I just didn't see the point anymore, in any of it. I was a failure for giving up my life plan of being a nurse. My friends all had brand-new sparkly lives, and I didn't hear from them anymore. I slept all the time, I hated school, and I was just 100 percent miserable. So I locked myself in the closet again and really, *really* started going at it with the cutting. And before I knew it my arms were covered in blood. As I sat bleeding, I remember thinking, *This is it. I am hopelessly, completely, absolutely crazy.*

I couldn't hide this one. I had to ask for help.

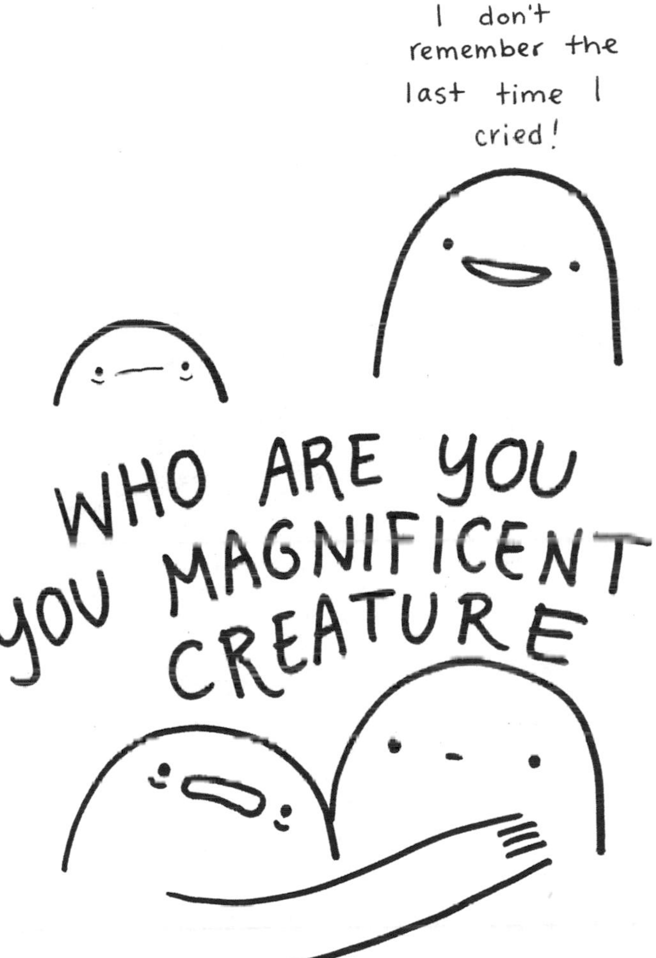
I don't remember the last time I cried!
WHO ARE YOU YOU MAGNIFICENT CREATURE

7

A sking for help is one of the hardest things you can do as a person.

It requires you to be vulnerable and appear less strong than you would like other people to think you are. It means letting someone into your world and allowing them to see the extent of the mess you are. But mostly it's a pain in the ass and not very fun.

The first time I really, truly asked for help, I was a scared and nervous freshman in high school. Adjusting to high school had been hard. My schoolwork was really challenging me; I was getting used to having different friends and, well, being a teenager. But mostly I was sad. Very sad. I wanted to not feel miserable all the time and for things to be different. So I decided to do what everyone says you should do: ask for help.

I walked into the guidance counselor's office at my school. "I think I need help," I said.

"With what?" the lady at the front desk said.

"Well, I'm sad all the time. I'm miserable and really upset."

"Oh," she said, looking at me with mild annoyance. "Well, we don't do that here. We do academic counseling, helping you pick classes and figure out your schedule. If you're having emotional problems, you should talk to your parents."

And she just looked at me like I was wasting her time. So I left.

I didn't tell anyone.

What was the point in reaching out for help if I was just going to be brushed off? And as wonderful as my parents are, what if they thought there wasn't anything wrong and I was being a crybaby? What if they judged me the same way the lady at the front desk did? These thoughts swirled in my head over and over. I didn't know what to do. So I did nothing.

This really enforced the wonderful process of Shoving Things Down and Pretending Everything Is Fine, Because Sharing Your Feelings Is Apparently a Bad Thing. I felt like I was bothering everyone by having any kind of problem. So I decided to have absolutely no problems. I did everything I could to distract myself from how awful I felt. Some days were tolerable, and some were even okay. But I couldn't get rid of the way I was feeling. And the more I ignored it, the deeper it sank.

Which eventually led to me sitting in my closet with my arms bleeding, absolutely convinced I was the craziest person to ever walk the planet.

Somehow, in that moment, the switch inside me flipped. I had parents. They were not the people at school or random strangers. I could talk to them. How many times had they told me, "If something is wrong, tell us"? Surely sitting in a closet covered in my own blood qualified.

I got up and walked to my parents' bedroom. I knew they were asleep and hated being woken up, but I went in anyway.

"Mom? Dad?"

"Mmmm."

"I need help."

"With what?"

"Well . . . everything."

My dad turned on the light, and my parents looked at my arms, then looked at my face. And something very fundamental shifted between us. They had known I was sad, that I wasn't adjusting to college well, but for the first time they really, truly, desperately understood how miserable my existence was.

My mom took me into the bathroom and cleaned my arms. My dad went through every room in the house, removing all sharp objects, even the tweezers. Fortunately, the cuts were not deep enough to warrant stitches, but my arms would have to be bandaged for a while. I crawled into bed with my mom and let her hold me, suddenly feeling very small and tiny, on the verge of being engulfed by the world.

My dad stayed up the whole night researching everything he could about depression.

And a new chapter began in my life, in all our lives: asking for help.

I'd like to tell you that I asked for help and everything immediately became 100 percent perfect, that I suddenly knew what I wanted to do in life, and that everything transformed into an absolute dream. But that's not how it works. Getting help is such a unique process in its own right, never quite

perfect, and progress is slow and something you're never really sure you're achieving.

We started with some small and significant changes: Tell Mom and Dad if you feel that upset again. See a therapist. Spend more time with the family. Pet a cat or a dog every now and then. Things got a little better, but not totally perfect. I took fewer classes than before, which relieved much of the academic pressure. When my friends called or texted me, I made an effort to respond, and the friendships that had drifted apart

Things aren't always perfect, but I'm here.

I'm better.

I'm me.

IT'S OKAY IF YOU FEEL
LIKE YOU'RE COVERED
IN THOUSANDS OF TINY
PIECES THAT WON'T
GO BACK TOGETHER RIGHT

YOU WILL FIND A WAY TO
MAKE THEM FIT, EVEN IF
IT DOESN'T LOOK ALL
PERFECT AND SHINY

got closer again. I began to open up to my mom and dad if things were feeling really bad. Slowly these changes started to help, and while things weren't exactly what I imagined, I was functioning again.

My depression moved all around over the next few years. Some moments were tolerable, some periods of time were unbearable, and some moments were honestly and truly okay. I worked with a multitude of therapists, took a lot more classes, and found I liked drawing things. I still struggled at times, with both depression and self-injury, but managed to stay afloat. Sometimes things felt bleak and bad, but I was still there. And I kept staying there.

And sometimes that's all we can really hope for—the feeling of staying afloat. When things really suck, staying afloat seems pretty good. Sometimes it's okay to celebrate just being here, because that in itself is an accomplishment. Some days I'm just going about my business, like walking around Target, and I'll think, *How on earth did I pick up all these broken shards and function like a normal person today?*

It's a mystery, I suppose, but sometimes those don't have to be solved.

PROGRESS IS PROGRESS, EVEN IF NO ONE NOTICES BUT YOU

RESISTED THE URGE TO LOOK UP PEOPLE YOU USED TO KNOW ☆

EFFORT WAS MADE

GOT BACK UP AND TRIED AGAIN EVEN THOUGH IT WAS HARD

SHARED FEELINGS EVEN THOUGH IT WAS A NIGHTMARE AND WAS BRAVE

FUNCTIONED A BIT!

DID SOMETHING NICE FOR YOURSELF

MADE AN APPOINTMENT AND WENT TO APPOINTMENT

YOU ARE AMAZING!

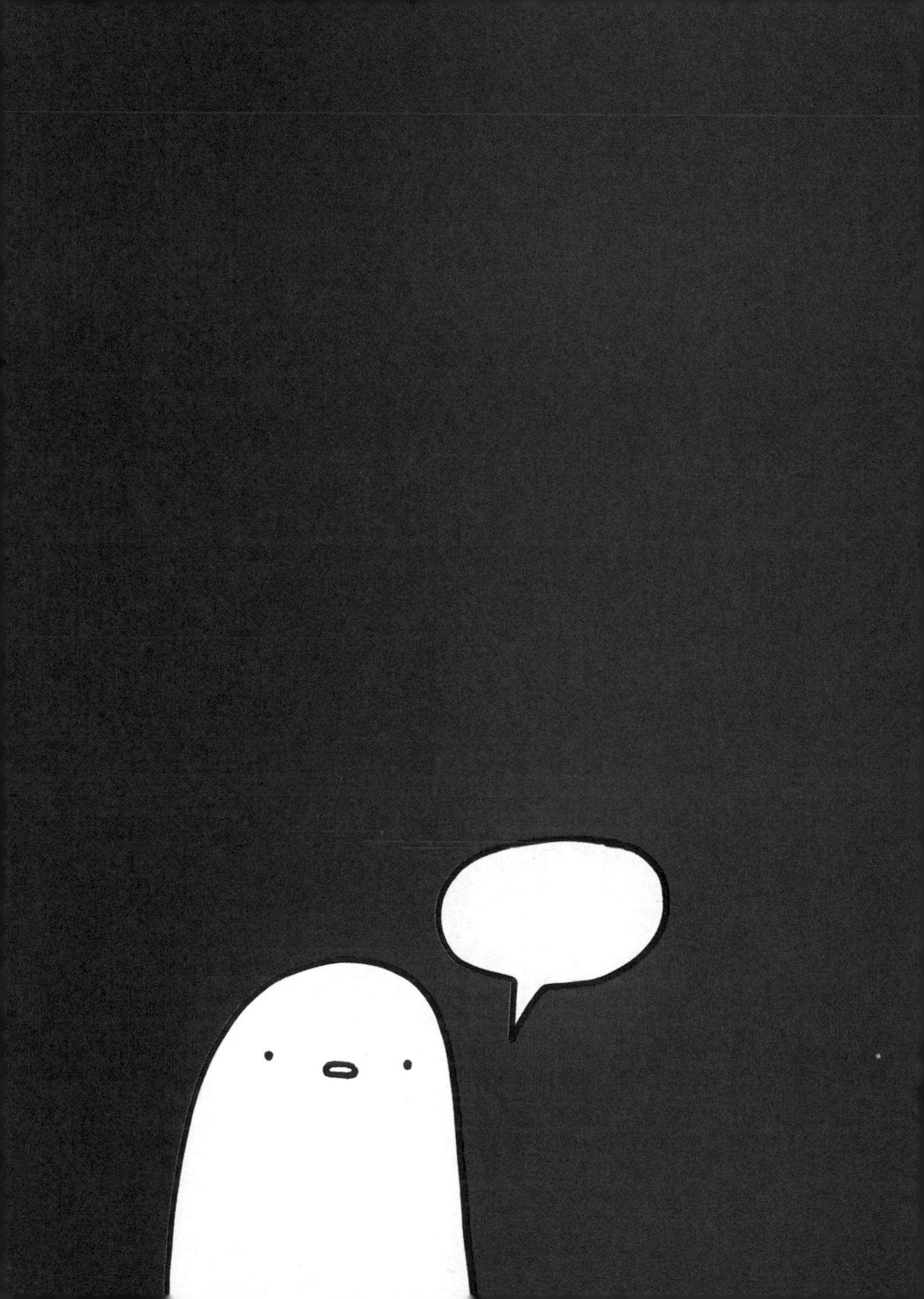

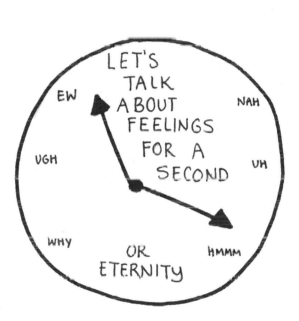

While choosing to ask for help can be life changing, it often feels like only half the battle. Talking to people you don't know? About *your* problems? Ugh. No matter whether it's your first time or tenth trip around, the prospect of talking to a professional about the hardest, messiest parts of yourself is difficult. Here are some ideas that might help.

Bring someone. If the thought of going by yourself to talk to a person you don't know about your feelings is scary and overwhelming, having a familiar face you trust with you can be a huge help. That person can also advocate for you or provide an outsider's objective view of how you're doing. In the past, when I have met a doctor, therapist, or psychiatrist for the first time, I've brought one of my parents, because sometimes I get nervous and forget what I wanted to say. The person you bring can remind you about what you meant to talk about if it slips your mind. And it's also helpful knowing you have someone you already trust in your corner as you attempt to trust a new person.

Don't show all your cards. Believe it or not, you don't have to tell a therapist everything about yourself at your first meeting. It's okay to just test the waters to see how they respond to minor problems or issues you might be having. Don't feel like you have to get down and dirty with your feelings on the first few visits, either—it's okay to go slow. If you feel comfortable sharing the smaller things, it will be easier to share the harder, tougher issues down the line. Building a relationship takes time, and it might take you a while. And that's totally all right.

Have multiple dates. It's okay if you don't feel like you and your therapist are a good match. If you were on a bad date, or didn't enjoy going out with someone after a series of dates, chances are you wouldn't keep going out with them. You can think of health care professionals the same way. If you really feel like the person you're working with doesn't understand your issues, who you are, what you need to get better, or, most importantly, *you*—you don't have to go back and see them. I once saw a therapist I didn't get along with because we seemed to fundamentally disagree on everything regarding how I should get better. I kept going to the sessions because I was convinced *I* was the problem, and it was only after she left the practice that I realized that maybe the issues with my progress didn't rest with me alone.

Nobody's perfect. Like with anyone else in your life, you're going to disagree with your therapist on some stuff. We all have arguments with our family and friends, and yeah, you might get into it with your therapist, too. This is okay and totally normal. It's good to hear what they think, but it's also okay to advocate for what's best for you. As long as you both respect each other and understand where the other is coming from, things will be fine. There's a difference between being annoyed with your therapist (like when mine said I didn't have enough charisma to be in the Spice Girls) and wanting to break up over something big and important (like the time I met with a therapist just once, but she talked over me the whole session and didn't listen to anything I said).

Advocate for yourself. If you really feel like things aren't going well, or that the therapist or doctor doesn't listen to or respect you, make a change. While therapy can be challenging, it shouldn't feel like a huge punishment every time you sit down on the couch. A good therapist should listen to you when you have concerns, and understand why something isn't working for you. I saw a therapist for a bit and I felt like I wasn't making any progress, so I expressed that. She understood my concerns and made adjustments to how she approached our sessions.

Sometimes there is this feeling that because the therapist is the professional, you can't ever question them or what they're doing. But since you're seeing them only in short doses, it's okay to want to make the most of that time, and want to be with someone who will respect you during it.

Therapy doesn't have to be forever. There seems to be this thought that if you have issues, a mental illness, or any kind of problem, you have to be in therapy for the rest of your life, forever, no early release. Therapy is just another tool that some people find helpful in getting better. It's not for everyone, but for some people it's essential. There were times when I found it extremely comforting and useful, and other times I've felt glad to not have it. It's a personal choice, and unless you have a court order to go or are in a hospital program, no one can make you. It doesn't have to feel like a life sentence—hopefully it will feel like something that helps make life a little more bearable. The important thing is that *you* choose the path that's right for you.

It's okay if things don't get better overnight. Sometimes change takes time. You're worth the investment.

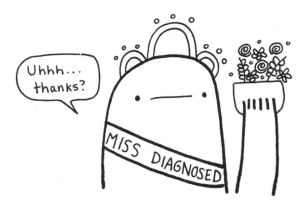

Uhhh... thanks?

MISS DIAGNOSED

I sat in a room and filled out all those little forms about myself.

Yeah, so you're bipolar.

Well, not the result I wanted but I'd face this head-on.

This meant...

medication

therapy

group therapy

And despite my best efforts, I was spiraling out of control.

My moods were all over the place and constantly shifting.

The medications weren't helping.

Therapy seemed impossible.

And group therapy wasn't doing it for me.

I was tired, I was not functioning, and I had now invested a year and a half into this bipolar diagnosis and was making zero progress — especially with the medications.

I was at the end of my rope.

I went back to my primary care doctor, who I trusted, and she suggested withdrawing from the medication to see how my body and mind reacted. She came up with a very safe and careful way to do this, and recommended we reevaluate in a bit.

I didn't notice
anything right
away,

but slowly I
was coming out
of my hibernation.

I was
interested in
little things
again.

These little things
kept building up
to me functioning.

I kept checking
in with my
doctor, and we
both agreed I
was making progress.

I had a
better
outlook on
things too.

As time went on,
we talked about
what might be
the problem overall.

Your moods are much
more stable but
you're still sad — it's
probably just depression
with your anxiety.

This made a lot more
sense to me, and we
came up with an
appropriate treatment
plan.

Sometimes it seems like mental illness is a competition,

like your symptoms need to be "bad enough" before anyone takes you seriously,

and when they remind you that "other people have it worse," it can be so upsetting.

When we pit our struggles against each other, it leaves no room for understanding or sharing experiences.

MY PROBLEMS

YOUR PROBLEMS

It closes the door to connections with people who could help us feel better — endlessly competing can even make things worse.

Just because someone experienced their problems differently doesn't make you or them any more or less worthy of validation.

They just had a different experience, and that's okay.

We can learn so much from each other.

All our experiences are real and valid.

The more we're in this together...

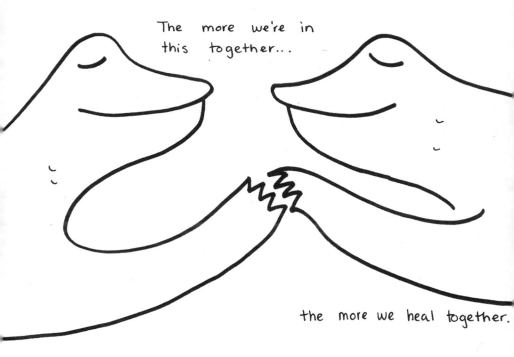

the more we heal together.

People often ask me —

WHAT DO YOU DO?

When I'm having a hard time with depression or anxiety, I can be totally sloppy with how I handle it. I'm far from perfect, but here are a few things that have helped me feel a little bit better.

MAP IT

I like to think of a big space, like a mall, a superstore, or even an airport, and "walk" through it in my head. I'm so engrossed in all the details (like where a door is) that I can calm down a bit. Works great before bed!

STATS:

Useless trivia becomes useful! Can you remember everyone who won an acting award, or which sports teams have won a tournament? List them in your head, become engrossed in the stats, and let the scary feelings take a back seat.

HEART TO HEART

If my heart is racing and out of control, I put my hand on my chest and feel how fast it's going — which encourages me to slow down my breathing. If I have a REALLY bad panic attack, my mom will match her breathing to mine so I slow down my breaths. A partner you can trust is really helpful!

DISTRACTION

It's okay to take a break for a bit! Watch TV, read, walk — just a little decompression can really help.

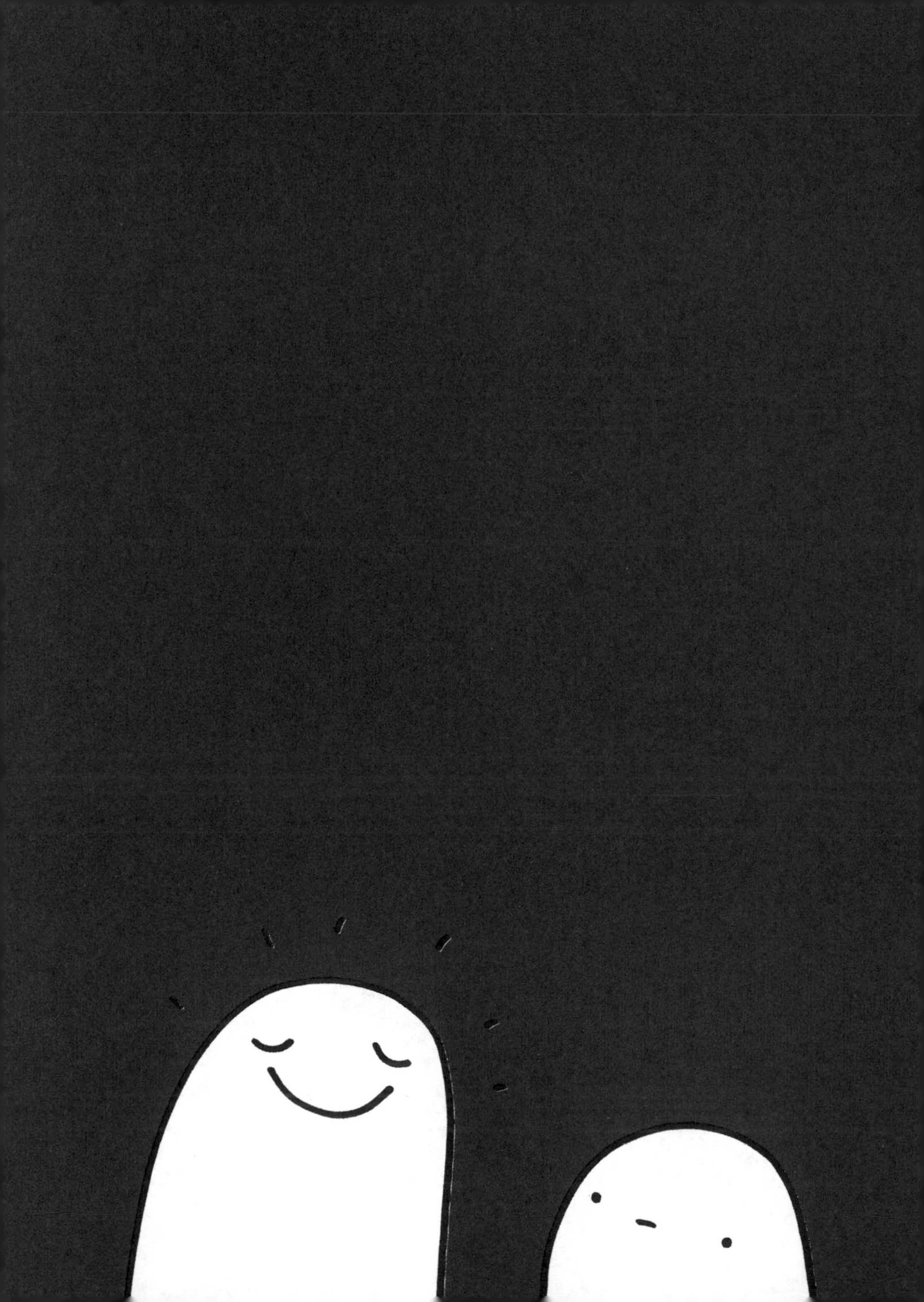

T hink positive and *be* positive!"
    "Have you tried yoga?"
"Happiness is a choice!"
"Honestly, if you just ate a healthy diet you'd feel great."
"Oh, and yoga. Do yoga!"
There's a good chance that if you have a mental illness, someone has tried to have this conversation with you. For some reason there are people on this planet who—once they figure

"HAPPINESS IS A CHOICE"

This is one of those phrases that drive me up the wall,

because depression IS NOT a choice — I don't wake up in the morning and actively decide to be sad.

People who are depressed definitely don't want to be, and are working hard to feel better.

They're definitely trying to be happy.

Acting like happiness is something you can pick up from the store like milk is totally soul crushing. Not to mention really unhelpful.

If someone is depressed and you want to encourage them, tell them they're doing a great job — happy or sad.

That kind of encouragement is a good choice.

out you're a little sad or anxious   feel they can pry into your life and tell you what to do. This is, of course, extraordinarily exhausting and annoying.

Some people who aren't depressed or upset feel that if you just strive for it enough, you can think yourself to happiness. Sadly, things don't work this way, and by the time you've heard a "just be positive" speech for the hundredth time, you're ready to whack that person with a yoga mat or shove some kale in their mouth to get them to shut up.

While the traditional sense of the word "positivity" is thinking good thoughts—and this does help many people—

94

for others that can seem daunting and a major challenge. Ultimately, though, positivity is a "positive" concept in that it can help center you and put the focus on what matters to you. That's the thing about positivity—no two people will ever have the same definition of it, and only you can create a definition that works for you. It's a unique and personal concept

UNWANTED MEDICAL
ADVICE AS BOOKS

that is tailored to each of us. You can't force your definition on someone else, and they can't force their definition on you.

And maybe some of the things that work for you don't quite match the cookie-cutter idea of "getting better." Maybe a really good bowl of cereal cheers you up, or perhaps you ditch the calming yoga mat for some intensive running. Finding what helps you feel better about yourself makes each day a little easier. It's important, great, and unique to you.

And that's pretty special, isn't it?

Self-love can be one of the hardest types of love to practice, because it can come with its own societal standards and contradictions, all of which can sometimes amount to intense pressure to *be* a certain version of yourself.

On the one hand, you have the traditional "perfect" standards—have a slamming body, nice hair, good teeth, and killer clothes. It's the quintessential body pressure, the norms you know you'll never live up to. But on the other hand, there's the body positive movement, which can be equally pressuring—love yourself *no matter what,* do what you want *no matter what,* embrace who you are *no matter what.* But what if you don't feel like you fall into either of these spaces? What if you're just kind of . . . there?

Honestly, I've struggled with my weight. I was always kind of chubby, but it never really bothered me. I had hang-ups about my body, like anyone else in high school, but with depression came overeating. And I'm not talking about eating a little more than I should have—this was me using food as a coping mechanism for my problems and gorging even when I felt sick. My weight began to skyrocket, but I didn't really notice or care. It just meant buying another size up at the store.

But my body began to notice and care. Just going up the stairs at home became exhausting. My legs hurt, I was tired all the time, and I had headaches. I would often have chest pain and nausea, and they woke me up at night. After weeks

of my jolting awake, clutching my chest and cringing in pain, my parents took me to the emergency room. The doctors did heart tests but found nothing wrong. They were, however, concerned about my weight. I was asked a lot of questions about

my diet, and for the first time I realized that my challenges had extended into overeating. I was depressed and using food to deal with my problems, which just made things worse. I had to make a change—not because of societal pressure, not because I failed at loving myself, but because if I didn't, I would just hurt myself even more.

"I HATE THE WAY
I LOOK SO MUCH"

WHAT PEOPLE THINK
I'M SAYING

Oh, I know
im okay, but
can you, like,
compliment me?

WHAT I AM ACTUALLY
TRYING TO SAY

I have literally refused to
leave the house because I
am so uncomfortable with
my looks.

My primary care doctor helped me set up a plan. Balanced meals, gentle exercise, and not reaching for food when I felt bad were my starting points. And it was hard. I started by walking around my neighborhood, but I never went too far. Meals were no longer endless plates of food. But it felt good to actively do something to improve my situation, instead of just sleeping again. When spring came I dusted off my old bicycle and started pedaling around. It was excruciating, like every muscle in my body was fighting me. But I liked getting out of the house to see what was happening around town. I began to go for a walk when I was upset instead of turning to food. I wasn't eating a lot of sugary or fried foods, either, because they slowed me down when I cycled. Slowly, slowly, it began to feel like I was making progress. The next time I visited my doctor, my weight wasn't even considered unhealthy anymore. The chest pain had disappeared, too.

The only problem was that I still hated the way I looked. It didn't matter that I had lost a lot of weight. I constantly found ways to be horrible to myself about my appearance. *Your stomach is still huge; cover it up. Wear a big baggy T-shirt. Your hips are too wide; better hide them. Your face looks awful today.*

My physical appearance had changed, but inside I was still the same—insecure and desperate to be accepted. There was the constant fear of *What if I put all the weight back on again and find myself miserable and depressed?*

Realistically, it's impossible to weigh the same amount forever. That's just not how our bodies work. Up, down, all

around—weight fluctuations are normal for humans. Learning to accept this and continue to *want* to take care of myself has been the real challenge—harder than any hill I have ever cycled up. It meant accepting that I was worth the investment of care.

IMPORTANT INFORMATION FOR

BEING HEALTHY

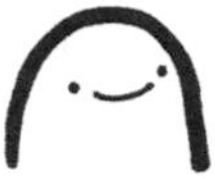

It's a very broad scale! "Healthy" means different things to different people, and it's all about how <u>you</u> do healthy.

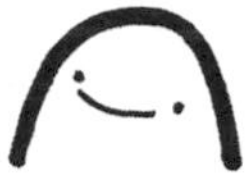

HEALTH ≠ WEIGHT

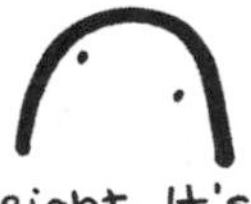

These are two different things – "healthy" does not mean you weigh a certain amount or that you have to reach a target weight. It's about taking care of yourself in a way that makes you feel good, both physically and mentally.

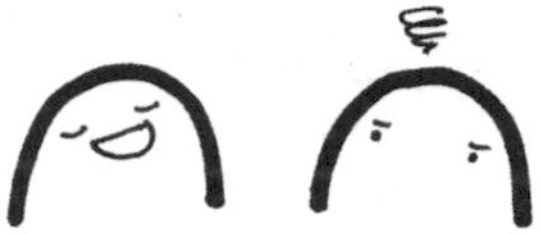

If someone pushes and pushes you to do exercise, you're probably not going to want to do exercise – it's a personal choice.

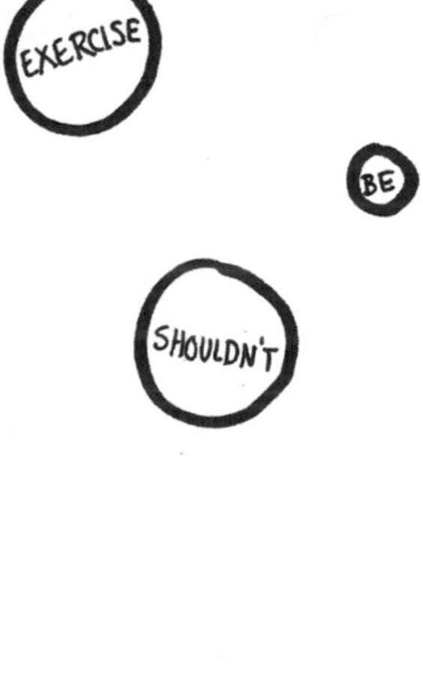

EXERCISE
BE
SHOULDN'T

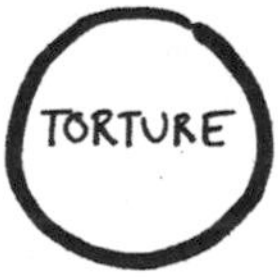

TORTURE

So many people act like the only exercise that "counts" is running. There are so many things to do that are exercise, like walking, gentle stretching, and anything that moves you. It's up to you!

HOW I GET DRESSED

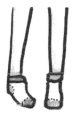

Legs, uh, better cover those up...

Stomach not flat! I should hide it.

Also I get weird about my arms and chest and sides and...

A walking censor block?

PERFECT!

We have all gotten a haircut we hate.

or put on clothes for the day that we regretted leaving home in.

The worst part is knowing someone will absolutely comment on it.

The key here is to LIE.

Act like you know what you're doing — confidence throws people off!

It's the latest style!

Then you may go home and hide under as many blankets as you like.

The thing is, no matter what you choose to do with your body—even if it's the best and absolute right decision for you as a person—it's going to be criticized. It will be looked at and thought about and be the subject of someone's opinion. It will be judged and scrutinized not only by other people, but by you. And that's a really hard reality to live with.

Someone will always stick themselves into your business and think they know best.

Someone will always make a comment about you gaining or losing weight and it will suck a lot.

Someone will always compare you to other people.

Someone will always make critical remarks.

Sometimes that someone will be you.

The key is knowing that you've made progress. Recognizing that progress, even if it's something very small—like ridiculously tiny, such as *I didn't gorge on food when I felt upset* or *Dammit, I am going to wear the tight leggings today*—is a victory.

Sometimes we get caught up in the idea that self-love has to be thinking we're great 100 percent of the time. Often it's something much less exciting, like treating ourselves with respect or holding our brains back a bit when we want to attack ourselves. In a world where we're taught to be one kind of perfect or another, sometimes seeing beauty in the imperfection is the best thing we can do.

BODY AWARDS

GOT MAD AT SELF OVER LOOKS BUT STILL WENT OUTSIDE ANYWAY

WAS FRUSTRATED ABOUT SELF-IMAGE BUT WAS ABLE TO GET ON WITH DAY

FELL BACK ON BAD HABITS THAT HURT SELF BUT ALSO AWARE THAT TOMORROW IS A NEW DAY

EXISTING (YES IT IS GREAT AND DESERVES AN AWARD!)

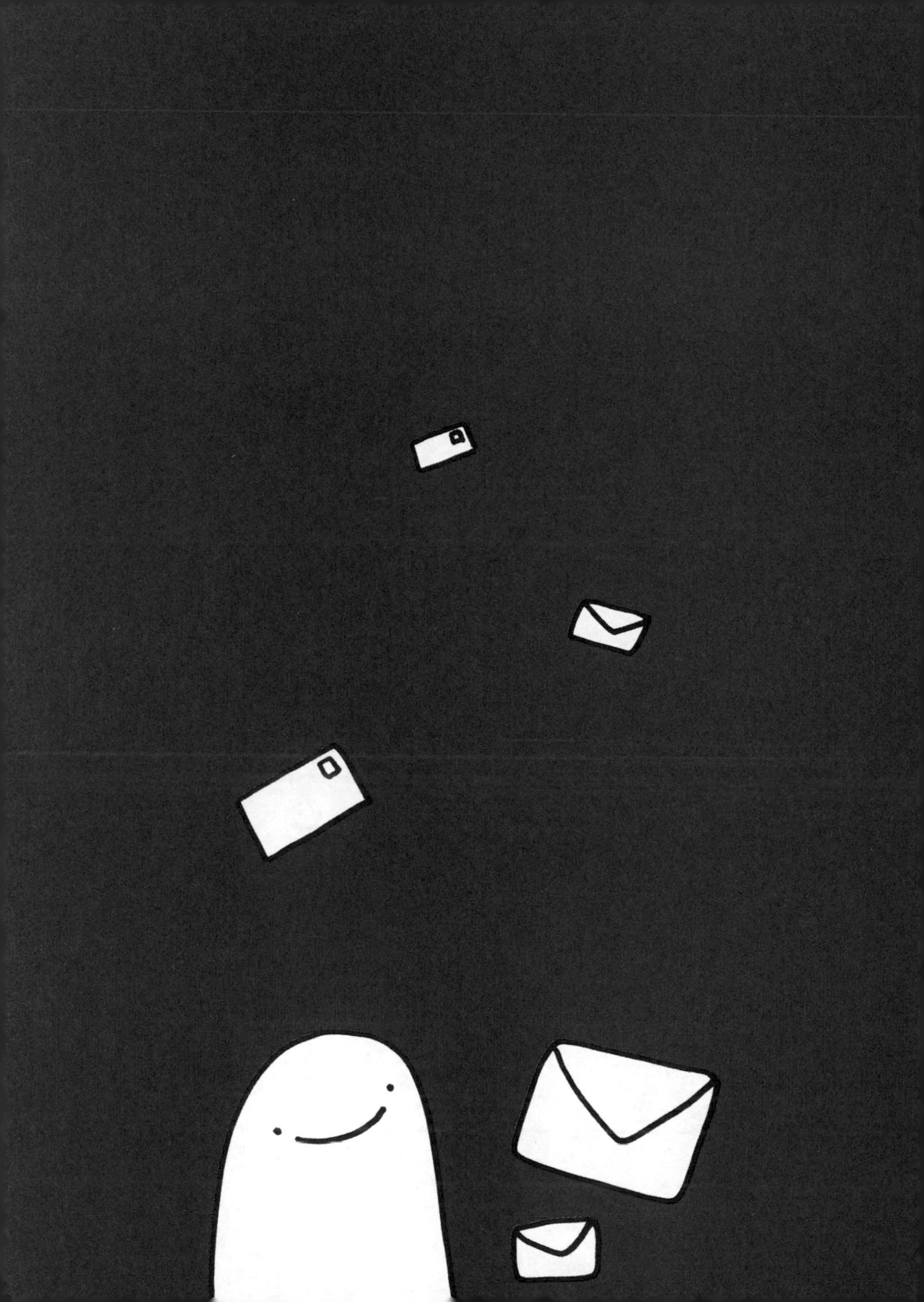

11

A lthough the internet can be a murky place, sometimes it can lead to friendships in the most unlikely places.

My friend Elisabeth is from Austria, and on the surface, we lead very different lives. She lives in Vienna and works in agricultural sciences, makes regular trips around the continent, and speaks a multitude of languages. Meanwhile, I live in the midwestern United States, I do drawings, and my English— the only language I speak—is sometimes questionable, at best.

And yet we are both utterly united in our love of the Eurovision Song Contest.

For those unfamiliar with the contest, Eurovision was started after World War II as a way to unite a broken continent through a night of song. What began as an extraordinarily classy affair later gave way to a three-night celebration full of glitter pop, wind machines, pyrotechnics, and dance music. While the contest is often regarded as cheesy, it quickly became a passion of mine after my cousin moved abroad. "Just watch it!" she begged. And once I did, there was really no going back. I now find I can relate to the masses who love sports, who follow the betting odds, eyes glued to their TVs. My sport just involves sequins and pop music.

The only downside to loving Eurovision is that it lacks a following in the United States. When my obsession began, the competition wasn't broadcast here, so there was no one to talk to about it. Thankfully the internet took care of that issue and introduced me to Elisabeth. I posted some drawings after Eurovision one year, and she sent me a casual message about

WHAT YOU NEED TO DO WELL AT EUROVISION

↑ more glitter

← glitter

a ball gown ↙

crazy ↙ hats

↑ wind machine

matching ↑ outfits

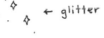

out-of-control prop ↙

↑ too much makeup

↑ your country's flag

an instrument ↙ you pretend to play

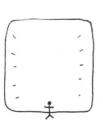

← a projected background that makes everything more confusing

↑ some kind of dance moves

← oh yeah! a good song!

the competition. Elisabeth was just as eager to find someone to talk to about Eurovision, and what started as small notes about our favorite songs that year quickly gave way to paragraphs about the contest. And soon those conversations changed from "Will the Czech Republic ever return?" to "What's it like going to school in Vienna?" Talking to someone thousands of miles away from you suddenly makes your everyday mundane life more interesting. While I was fascinated to hear all about daily life in Europe, Elisabeth was equally interested in what it was like in America. We ended up exchanging addresses and sending each other postcards, which led to gifts on holidays and, well, actual friendship.

Internet friendship is its own type of friendship, because internet friends are not involved in your daily life. Rather,

I worry a LOT about how other people view me.

Like oh my gosh, if I'm into things and other people don't like those things as much as I do, does that mean they don't like ME?

So the more I like things, the more I keep them locked up.

STUFF I LIKE DO NOT OPEN

It kind of makes me dizzy, constantly calculating what I can share about stuff I like without putting too much of myself out there.

But when I do feel comfortable letting people in,

it's pure magic,

and so worth it!

they get bits and pieces of it—and you get to choose which bits and pieces you present to them, which can take some pressure off initially. But I eventually learned that as with in-person friendship, it's okay to show weakness at times, and doing so can help deepen the relationship.

After I had a hard time with depression, I did a bit of writing about it online. About a week later I got a package in the mail from Elisabeth. She wanted to cheer me up, so she sent me all kinds of newspaper clippings about our favorite Eurovi-

sion stars, some chocolate, and a note. I actually cried because
no one had ever just sent me something in the mail because
they were thinking of me! It was a whole new way to look at
having a friendship with someone.

"Douze points" is French for "twelve points"—the highest
score a song can get. I would give this friendship douze points
for sure. Although we are separated by an ocean, a continent,
and the mountains of western Austria (my geography of Eu
rope is stellar now), I feel like Elisabeth is a real-life friend.
It's great having someone in my email just to talk to about
this silly song contest we love so much. And although every
year a new group of people take the stage to battle it out with
weird props and electro beats, it's cool that I'm dependably in
sync with someone halfway across the world. Mostly, it's nice
knowing that a friend thousands of miles away thinks that
I'm pretty okay as a person.

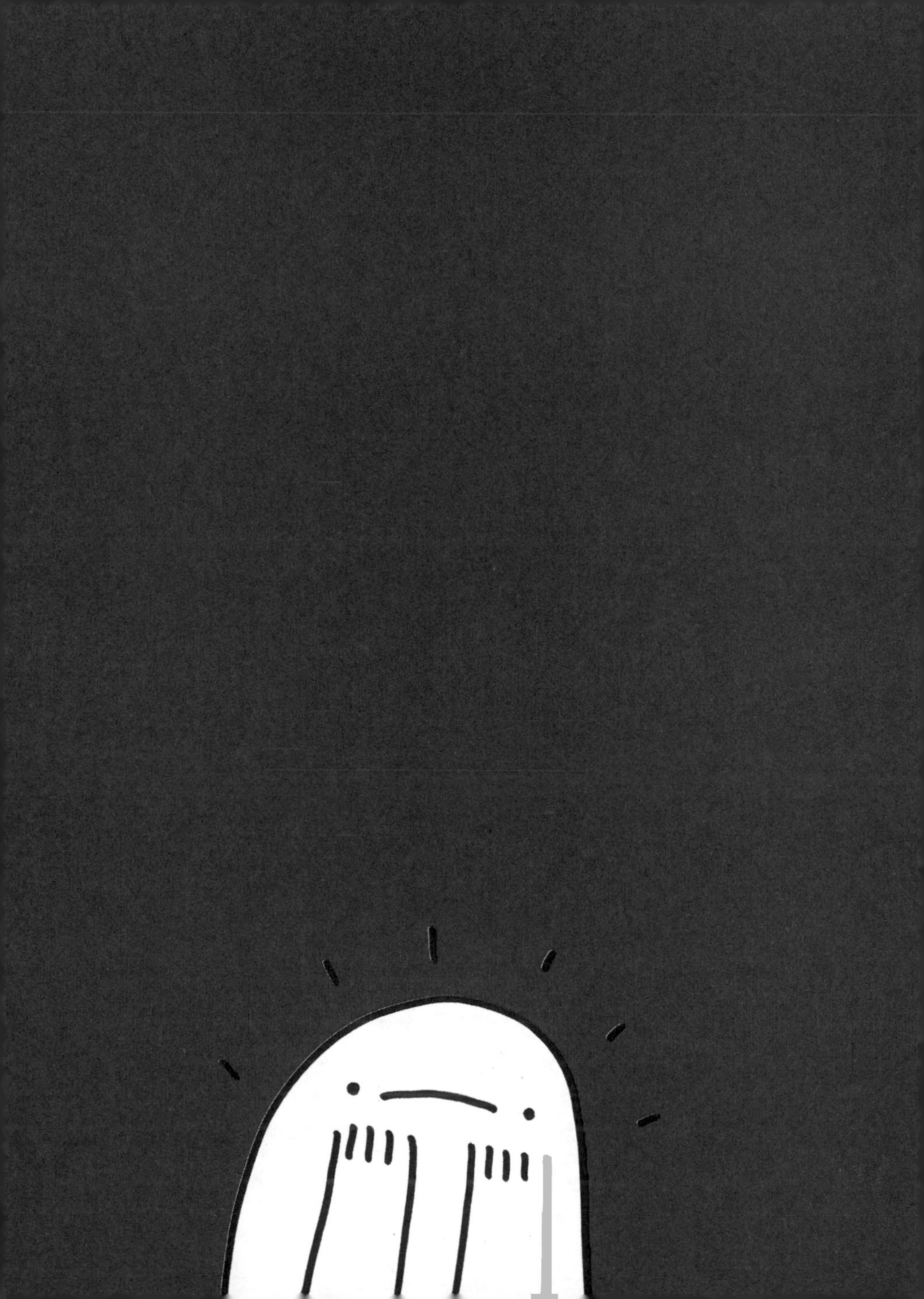

12

Recently, I was invited to a graduation party for my friend's sister. It was a large affair, with tables full of delicious home-cooked food and lots of laughter. Although I tend to get nervous at these sorts of things, the sun was shining and I felt fairly at ease. As I made my way through the throngs of people chatting away, I was relieved to see that my group had broken off into our own table, which included my friend's cousins, who were visiting from Canada. I had met these cousins multiple times before, so I even felt comfortable around them.

As afternoon turned into evening, we became known as the twenties table, as we were all young adults and were surrounded by either real grown-ups or teenagers. The conversation was surprisingly smooth, and I was enjoying myself.

Until someone mentioned Justin Bieber.

"Oh," I said, looking at the Canadian cousins. "I keep forgetting he's your responsibility."

I regretted the words the moment they left my mouth. I didn't have anything against the guy, and certainly didn't mean anything by them, but they slipped out anyway.

"WHAT?" said one of the cousins.

"He's just a good Canadian boy who was corrupted!" cried the other.

"*You* gave us Miley Cyrus!" added the first.

Before long the whole table was in an uproar about who gave who what, cake forks pointing as accusations flew about Avril

Lavigne, and jaws dropped at the revelation that both Ryan Gosling *and* Ryan Reynolds are Canadian. As entertaining as it was, the tension was rising and my stomach was sinking—I had single-handedly destroyed diplomatic relations between the United States and Canada.

I tried to apologize, but my pleas went unheard as someone shouted, "WHAT ABOUT DRAKE?" Fortunately, just as everyone began to dig in their heels, someone brought up how expensive it is to move out, and we were suddenly united over the fact that no one our age on the North American continent can afford a house.

International relations are truly a beautiful thing.

But when I got home that night, the echoes of the bickering still played in my head. Even though rationally I knew the stakes were low, I still couldn't help but wonder *why* I had to open my stupid mouth and make that comment. I turned a perfectly good dinner into a petty free-for-all argument. It's not like I'd never see those people again. What if the cousins now thought I was a sarcastic jerk? What if they hated me for it? What if they got my address from my friend and showed up in the night to throw Tim Hortons coffee at my bedroom window, even though I rationally knew they were very nice and would never do that?

There are two separate parts when you screw up in front of other people: the actual event and the aftermath in your

head. When you say something stupid to someone else, there's a really good chance it's not a big deal to them, although it can often feel like the whole world is ending to you. There's a high probability that someone's said something idiotic to you, and then apologized or tried to make amends. When that happened, could you even remember what they said to you?

Probably not.

But when it's us, our brains just make everything a million times worse, convincing us that even if we apologized and everyone is totally cool, we still *MADE A MISTAKE* and must monitor all future behavior to ensure nothing like this ever happens again. But these things keep happening because we're human, and it's in our nature to screw up, especially at

Honestly I am so bad at conversation and have screwed up so badly that I am going to need constant reassurance that I am okay as a person.

I'm the kind of person who spends way too much time dwelling on the past — I just can't seem to let stuff go,

especially if I did

something

BAD.

You see, "bad" to me means lots of things, but mostly that I might have hurt someone.

This could take the form of:

A) something I said
B) joke gone wrong
C) something I did

The good news is that I get to agonize for eternity about what people think!

I'm always convinced people will remember and everyone will hate me and think I'm awful.

BREAKING NEWS

THAT THING YOU HOPED YOU'D FORGET IS STILL ON YOUR MIND!

PERSON MADE FRIEND MAD IN 2009

HURTFUL ACTION STILL REMEMBERED

And hey, letting go of stuff is hard - it's no easy feat!

This is because I am caught between the past and now - the past, where I may have done something bad,

PAST   NOW

and the now, where I haven't.

The key is to pick the now - not only because you live here, but because if you are hyper-worried about past behavior, chances are you are making different choices now.

Like

good

choices.

PAST   NOW

Every day is a chance to start fresh with your choices, and to be the you that YOU want to be.

The past may creep up and remind me I'm awful,

but I'm choosing the now each and every time.

parties and social functions when there's a lot of interacting happening at once. Yet there's a difference between making mistakes and being a bad person. Making a mistake is saying something careless, embarrassing, or crass. Being a bad person is actively trying to hurt others.

People can sense the difference between the two, even if you think they can't. Chances are that tomorrow no one will even remember the ridiculous thing you said, and they certainly wouldn't think any less of you (especially if you apologize).

The easy part of screwing up is saying you're sorry and having someone say they're okay with it. The hard part is forgiving yourself and recognizing that it's okay to let go of these little infractions. No one is perfect. If we were perfect, there would be no one to argue over the Canadian Ryans, and what kind of world would that be?

13

THE PASS

The first day of high school was always notoriously boring. It was the ultimate mundane routine, where teachers just droned on about the course materials and everyone forgot how long the day actually was. At least after all this time of pushing myself academically, I could finally afford to take a class for fun in the fall of my senior year. I had chosen Music Appreciation, and while I didn't know what I was getting into, I thought it might be interesting. On the first day, our teacher walked into the room wearing a shirt for a band I didn't know. Another student immediately started talking to him about it, and they seemed completely engrossed in the conversation. I asked them about the band, and they recommended a couple of songs to me.

When I got home I skimmed the track titles and decided to give them a listen. But as I was shuffling through, the opening of a song caught me, and by the time the song finished, my face was streaked with tears. Isolation, feeling like I didn't exactly belong, the looming future—the music was mirroring my personal experiences. The song was called "Subdivisions," the band was called Rush, and something inside me just felt connected to them both. I kept clicking on song after song, completely enamored.

Rush was the ultimate misfit band. They were ridiculed by the mainstream press, chastised for being too complex or uncool. But I found something I liked in their music. And the more I read about the fans who liked them, the more the

WHY RUSH?

If you're anything like my parents, you're probably wondering why a teenage girl got super into a band whose primary fan base is men in their 50s and older. Let's examine this!

GEDDY LEE bass, vocals, keyboards
Basically he's a mind-blowing multitasker

ALEX LIFESON
guitars

Known for his amazing solos — and his sense of humor

NEIL PEART
drums, lyrics

A legend at his instrument, but just as skilled with words

THE MUSIC

Complex, technical, and includes a wide variety of styles. But mostly it's interesting, and I really liked that.

THE THINKING

I liked being challenged by the music to read or try new things. It encouraged me to learn and explore more.

THE LYRICS

Lots of songs about mythology, philosophy, literature, science, human nature, communication — and even robots. I always got something new when listening.

THE FANS

Plenty of people who felt like they didn't belong — and I managed to fit right in.

music resonated. The band created common ground across generations for people like me, who felt like they didn't fit in.

I don't know if it's because I was unwaveringly nice to people or because I cried so easily, but I was always a prime target for bullies. I could never understand what I was doing so wrong—all I wanted was to be a part of the community. It was so unbearable in junior high that I almost changed schools, but I decided to stick it out because high school was right around the corner. Things had to get better, right?

Sort of. Sometimes people left me alone, and other times I got hurt pretty badly. I had endured being ganged up on and ridiculed to the point of tears on my sixteenth birthday and dealt with vicious rumors, but my greatest challenge was the boy who sat next to me in my science class. His reason for picking on me? *I took the bus.* It was by far the stupidest thing I had ever been bullied for. But his endless taunts about how I didn't have my own car escalated to jabs about everything wrong with me as a person, and it really got to me. My heart sank lower and lower each morning as the bus pulled up to the school, because I knew he'd see me. I even asked my teacher for help, but was met with a very sage "I don't get involved in my students' problems; he probably just likes you." I couldn't escape my bully during class, but I was

MORNING ESSENTIALS

some level of
coffee in
a
thermos

industrial
↙ backpack
because
it is
school

↑
sunglasses to hide
how anxious I look

← CD player with all
of my favorite music

BRING
IT ON,
BULLIES

hell-bent on escaping the bus. I would do anything to get him off my case.

So I started riding my bike to school, even though it meant getting up very early, pedaling for miles, and waiting endlessly on corners for traffic to pass.

I had my bike, my headphones, and a selection of Rush CDs, which made the mornings more bearable. As the weather got colder, I bundled up in scarves and rotated the discs. On the days when the weather forced me to take the bus, I cranked up the music, determined to walk into the building and get on with the day, headphones blaring every time I went into the science room.

And you know what?

It *worked.*

He left me alone.

What was so fantastic about Rush's music was that it allowed me to escape into my own world for a while, free from feeling like a failure at school, free from the taunts, free from the uncertainty of it all. The music enveloped me, and the lyrics spoke to my sad teenage self, as well as to sides of me I didn't even know I had yet. I didn't really talk about it with anyone. The minute you start to mention that you listen to music from a different generation than your own, you are immediately tied down to a chair and forced to name three albums, ten obscure songs, and the social security numbers of the band members. I wasn't interested in playing that game, so I kept my interest in Rush's music to myself. All I ever really wanted was to be normal, to feel like I belonged. And yeah, maybe I was being bullied, which made things hard. But perhaps feeling *understood* by this band could be an acceptable substitute for that feeling of belonging.

Feeling wholly and completely understood by people who don't know you personally is a very powerful thing. Oftentimes through songs, books, and movies, we are reminded that our feelings are universal and that we're not alone in this life. Everyone has their own thing that speaks down to the depths of their soul, soothes them, and picks up their broken pieces on bad days. It's amazing to feel so connected from such a distance.

People like to hear that what keeps you going is your family, your friends, and your future. But when times are bad, the things that sustain you probably aren't going to be the sunshine and daisies they're expecting. It's more likely to be something small and totally insignificant in the grand scheme of things. It might be something that you can't physically touch, like a movie, a television show, a book, or music,

... And then there is me.

Whoops...

Rush has a very passionate fan base, and many pride themselves on how many times they saw the band live.

I always had two big problems— first, no one ever wanted to go with me

and later, my anxiety was so bad I stopped doing concerts entirely.

So when the last tour ever was announced for 2015, this was it. But I was just coming out of a 2-year depression, and only functioning a little bit.

Wanna go see Rush?

No.

Okay, can't go by myself so I won't go at all.

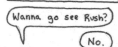

Everything is loud and confusing and I am freaking out so much!

HELP ME!

I just wasn't ready for something like this again.

For a long time, I was mad at myself for missing out — I never got to see them play live! It was a total regret that just ate at me.

But the regret eventually faded because by not going, I'd avoided putting myself in an unnecessarily stressful position during a fragile time.

I should have sucked it up and gone!

Ugh, why didn't I just go?!?

Ugh!

I took care of myself and let myself just get better

and that's really okay!

All that regret lit a fire in me. I was tired of sitting out of everything and missing experiences. I wanted to do things!

But the more I did both big and little things, the easier it got to do anything.

This isn't fun, but hey. I'm not crying so far.

Because I took so much time to really get a grip on my anxiety, I knew how to handle it if I broke down. While I regret not getting to see Rush live, I don't regret taking care of myself.

We got this!

Totally!

BIG BOX OF COPING SKILLS

The first few outings went as expected. Dread the day of the event, panic at the event, nausea, antianxiety meds, and lots and lots of tears...

Why did I do this?

I'm so miserable!

Until it eventually became a good time!

I'm glad we did this, I'm having such a blast here!

And if they're ever ready to tour again...

EMERGENCY RUSH FUND

I'll be ready, too.

leaving you feeling completely held together by a piece of media. For me, it was listening to "The Pass" about a hundred times in a row, feeling like *"turn around and walk the razor's edge"* was my lifeline. Anything that's important to you is just as vital as any therapy session or talk with your friends. It's like an invisible thread keeping you tethered to the world. And it should be celebrated that you found something to keep you going, no matter what it is. Because the more you go, the more things fall into place. Whatever your medium is, it's another great piece in the puzzle of moving forward.

Although I missed my chance to see Rush live, I did get an opportunity to do something related to the band. There was a documentary coming out about the final tour called *Time Stand Still,* and it was being shown for one night in theaters. I grabbed tickets immediately and started counting down the days to my very first Rush-related activity. And when the day came, I got there early and had such a thrill seeing everyone in their concert shirts. The people were young and old, men and women, and everyone looked as pleased as I was to be there. I listened around me, and the crowd in the theater echoed the same feelings I had—they felt like they had never fit in, and that this was their *thing.* I even made small talk with the couple sitting next to me. And as the theater darkened, the audience cheered. The screen got bright, but not as bright as the smile on my face.

Because I felt like I belonged.

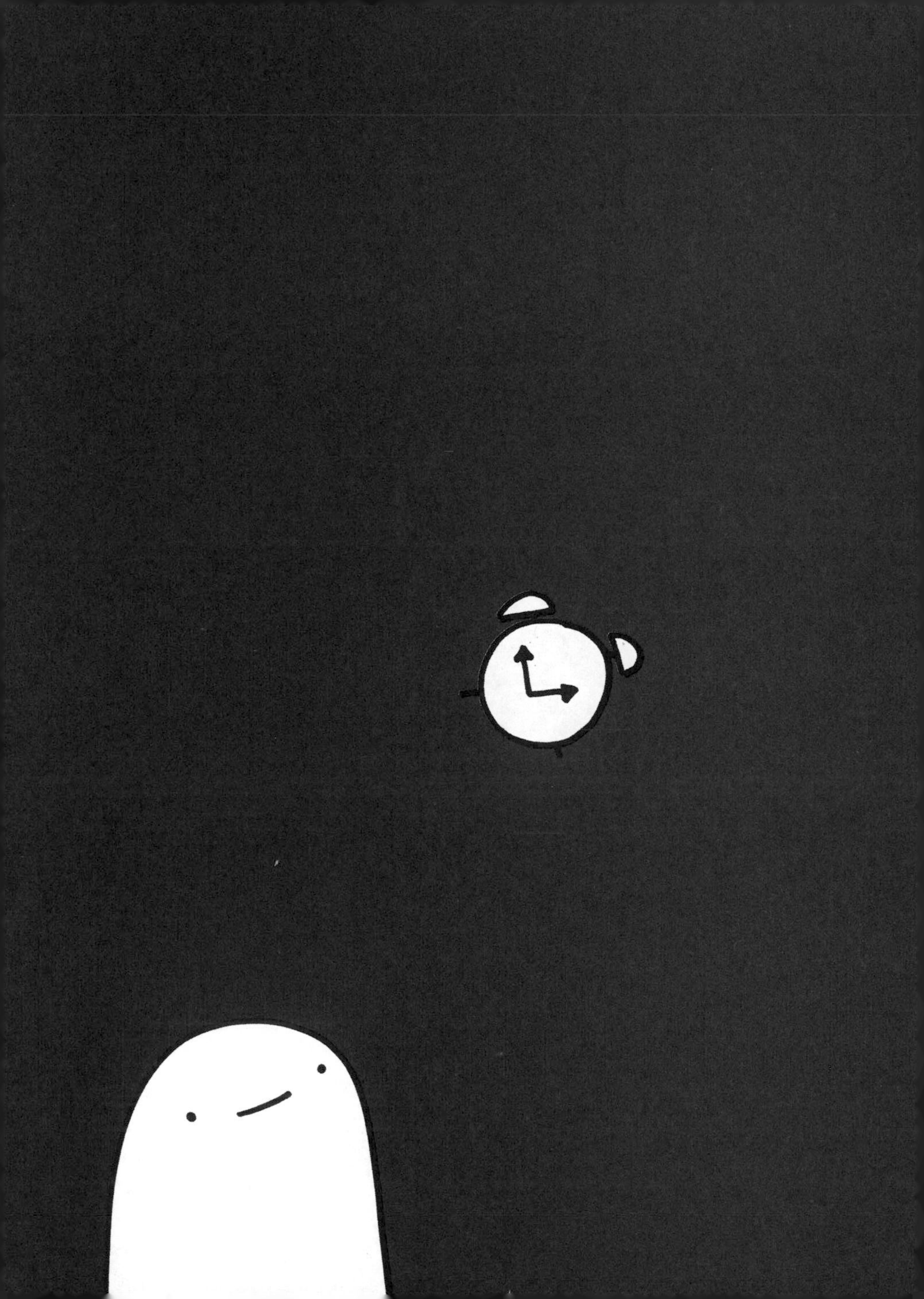

14

If you were bullied a lot growing up, sometimes it can be really difficult to move past that. The taunts, teasing, and harassment are all things I still struggle with today. When people have hurt you for a long time, it can be hard to feel like you've made any progress. It's difficult being torn between who you were when people hurt you and who you are now—especially when the two cross over. Sometimes the full scope of bullying isn't understood by other people, almost as if "bullying" just means "someone said something mean once," instead of encompassing the actual damage it inflicts. Here's a quick guide to what I've learned from being bullied.

It's definitely not you. I used to think all the reasons I was being bullied were my fault. I wore glasses, I didn't look cool, I liked weird things. It was easier to absorb this as being my problem, not the bullies'. And it was even easier to believe that everything they said was true. I would ask myself, *What did I do to make them hate me so much?* But I didn't do anything. I just existed. And I didn't deserve horrible treatment. No one does! Being who you are, liking the things you like—those are fantastic. And it's so sad everyone can't see the beauty in that, because it really is beautiful.

It affects your future relationships. Because bullying is a social thing, it's really affected how I interact with people.

Sometimes people just don't see bullying as a big deal,

like "Oh, it happened in the past, someone said something mean once."

But when you were a frequent target for awful stuff, it's much more than that.

It can really affect you years later, and it's okay to acknowledge that.

There's nothing that says you have to "get over" it by a certain time or date.

STORM OF BULLYING

No matter what happened, your feelings are real and valid.

You'll make progress in your own way in your own time.

You've got this!

If someone is being nice to me, I'm convinced it's because they have secret motives and are actually teasing me, and if someone gently makes a joke at my expense, I've been known to take it really personally. I went through years of people being nice to my face but actually making fun of me behind my back, and it's something I'm still figuring out how to unravel. Focusing on the positive relationships I do have has helped immensely. And those relationships don't even have to be traditional ones—my relationship with my plants has been great, because they don't say bitchy things when I'm not there. It's okay if you still struggle with social interaction because of bullying. You'll get there.

"Bullies are usually bullied themselves." You probably heard this from various adults when you were a kid. Because things aren't bad enough; now you're supposed to be all sympathetic to the people who hurt you and to magically produce understanding and forgiveness. People outside the situation love to turn it around so it doesn't require them to deal with the actual issues. After all, it's easy to forgive and forget, right? While it's good to think about other people, in a situation where you are being repeatedly hurt, it's okay to want to just focus on yourself and your feelings. Forgiveness can come when you're ready, if it ever comes at all. That's up to no one but you.

Disconnect and unplug from the past. Don't be their online friend, and don't read their pages, blogs, accounts, feeds, their dogs' pages, whatever. Even if they've changed, it just dredges up old memories. The less attention you pay to them, the better you'll feel. It can be tempting to rejoin online groups or sneak a look at their photos, but it just starts a cycle of misery. Trust me on this one. I've done this and then gotten horribly anxious about things that happened years ago and spent the night crying my eyes out. It's not worth the upset.

Bullies exist in all parts of life. Even into adulthood, there are people who enjoy knocking down others for fun. It's usually more subtle, through backhanded compliments, rude remarks, and gossip. Some people just like hurting others. And with social media, it's more vicious than ever. Everyone likes to say "Don't pay attention to the trolls," but it's very hard to pretend that someone's amazingly hurtful comment didn't affect you. It's okay to acknowledge that it does. And sometimes it's okay to realize some people are just horrible!

Things do get easier. It's one of those ridiculous sayings that means nothing to you when it's happening, but feels true later. When I was younger and being hurt, people used to tell me it wouldn't matter one day, and that it would stop. It felt like such a joke at the time—how does thinking about the future help me now? What helped me focus and get through were books, music, the friendships I did have, and constantly drawing. But what helped most of all was time. Putting time and space between myself and the people who hurt me gave me the ability to move on. Now that I'm here, life isn't always what I imagined. Mean people still exist, but it's easier to ignore them. The people who are actually okay more than make up for them. I have a tight-knit group of friends and a job I love, and I don't think about the people who hurt me every day.

And I think that's progress.

BULLIED!

Freaked out about everything I say and do, afraid of always having a target on my back.

"They picked on me, so there must be something wrong with me."

"I am going to do everything differently and hide anything I actually care about and never show emotion again."

(TIME PASSES)

Realize that this was not my fault, but rather someone else's, and that it's okay just to be me.

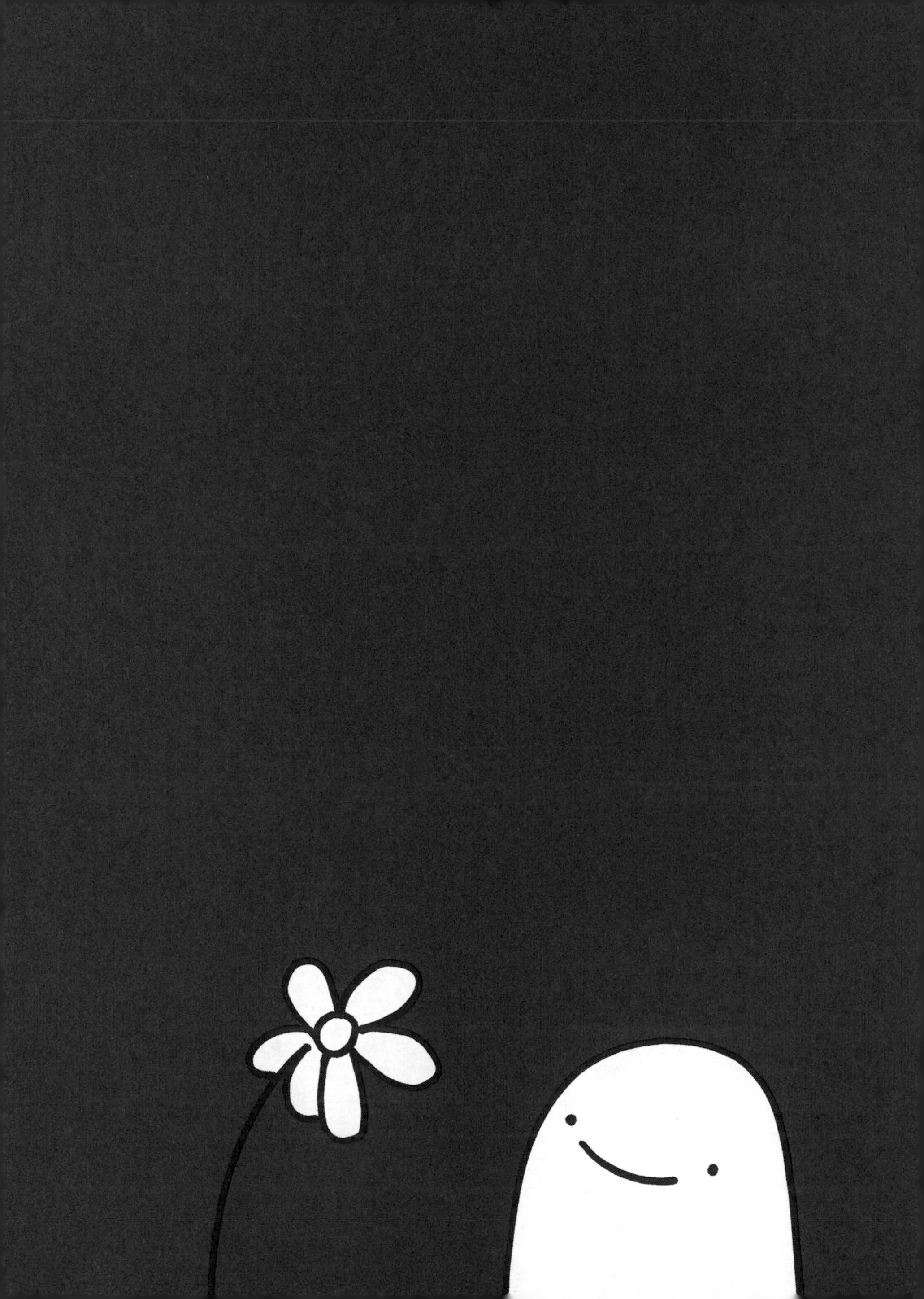

YOU'RE OKAY - - - - -

- - - PROMISE - -

15

I think one of the hardest sentiments to wrap my head around is that I'm an all right human being. So often my brain screams that I'm the worst of the worst, and I constantly judge myself for past interactions and failures. I also need constant reassurance from those around me that I'm not a horrible person, which, honestly, is grating for everyone involved.

I get wrapped up in my thoughts that I need to be a good person. But my brain gives me so many warped definitions of what a good person must be that it's almost a moot point. *A good person must never say or think anything that could be offensive. A good person must be good every minute of their life and never make anyone upset. A good person must never do* anything *bad.* While I do worry how other people see me, the standards for "good" I'm chasing are arbitrary and created by my anxiety.

There aren't any set standards of what makes a "good" person. This is both frustrating (how do I be one?) and helpful (well, I guess I can be my own kind of good). The thing is, we're often so caught up in worrying whether we're okay that we don't even notice we already are, and that we actively do good in our daily lives. Have you ever cheered up a friend? Sent a funny text to someone because you thought of them? Picked up litter on the sidewalk? Smiled at a dog? All these actions are positive ones, and they probably made someone (including the dog) happy. It's also important to make sure *we're* happy. Self-care is so unique and important and vital to our well-being. It's good to remember to take care of ourselves,

There's often a lot of pressure to be a certain kind of person— to be a flawless, "perfect" human.

It's like there's this list of things people expect from me. I don't think I can check them all off.

- SMART
- ATTRACTIVE
- PERFECT AT STUFF
- LIKES THE RIGHT THINGS

That's because lists like this are unrealistic.

But there is a right way to be a person...

... it's by being yourself.

A BIG THING OF
REMINDERS

Most of the time depression feels like the end of the world, but it's not — there is a lot of world that is definitely not ending!

People really like recovery to have a time-table, but in reality it may take a while, and that's okay! You're worth the time and energy it takes to get better.

Things take time to change, and every small bit that goes well is a step toward that. And all the little steps add up to bigger and bigger leaps. And when life begins changing, you might not even notice.

Because you're too busy actually living.

Self-care can sound overly complex with, like, a hundred requirements,

but it's really whatever you want it to be! Is there something that helps you feel better? That's self-care!

you might feel like you've been stuck in the here and now for an eternity, and that moving on into the future will never come. Although time passes slowly, things will change — maybe not exactly how you envisioned, but they will change.

SMALL EFFORT

MEDIUM EFFORT

LOTS AND LOTS OF EFFORT

Being kind to yourself can be very difficult, and is often best practiced in small doses. It's okay if you can't do it right away! Inside or out, all parts of you are great.

You're a total champion for dealing with your mental health! So often we don't acknowledge how hard it is to get up and deal with it on a daily basis, and doing so is really incredible!

Go you!

It's okay if you struggle with returning to life 100% after things go really wrong. Sometimes the greatest challenges are the little things, like conversations and grocery shopping. You are on the right track, and in time these things won't seem as daunting.

You're great. Promise. Anyone who spends so much time worrying about social interaction, how they appear to other people, and what they say _cares_ about people. And when you care, people do notice that, and that makes you great!

"Just be yourself" is advice lots of people give, but not many of us practice. Letting people in can be hard! But sharing little pieces of ourselves can make it easier, and when we do let people we trust see who we are, it's very rewarding.

RESOURCES

Remember: no problem or issue is too insignificant for you to reach out for help!

UNITED STATES + CANADA

NATIONAL SUICIDE PREVENTION LIFELINE

1-800-273-8255
suicidepreventionlifeline.org

THE TREVOR PROJECT

1-866-488-7386
thetrevorproject.org

TRANS LIFELINE

1-877-565-8860
translifeline.org

HALF OF US

halfofus.com

UNITED KINGDOM + IRELAND

SAMARITANS

116 123
samaritans.org

MIND

0300 123 3393
OR TEXT 86463
mind.org.uk

SANE

0300 304 7000
sane.org.uk

AUSTRALIA AND NEW ZEALAND

AUSTRALIA

LIFELINE

13 11 14
lifeline.org.au

BEYONDBLUE

1300 22 4636
beyondblue.org.au

NEW ZEALAND

SAMARITANS

0800 726 666
samaritans.org.nz

This is a short list of resources, but there are plenty more online!

You can find help 24/7/365 from all around the world.

You definitely aren't alone, and the sooner you ask for help, the sooner you can feel
: better :

too, because the people we take care of would want that for us! We tend to forget that other people view us so differently from how we view ourselves.

So take pride in who you are, who you love, what you love, and the intangible things you can't touch but still love. These are all amazing. Be kind to others, be kind to animals, and don't forget to be kind to yourself. The world can always use more kindness. You're never alone in this life, and your feelings echo through the generations. You have an impact, a voice, and one that deserves to be heard. Moments of trouble may come and cloud your life, but you will always manage to shine through, even if it's the most difficult thing in the world. People can see the good in you, even if you can't always see it for yourself.

But most importantly, you're okay.

Promise.

The cool night breeze blew strands of my hair into my face, and I was already having a hard time seeing. I nervously tucked them back and stayed crouched and huddled. Twigs and leaves jammed into my sides, and I could barely see my friend Katie at the altar. It was her wedding, my stomach was filled to the brim with anxiety, and I was hiding in a bush. How did I get here? Let's back it up a little bit.

Weddings are nerve-racking for everyone, because they involve formal wear, conversation with strangers, and dancing. I was nervous to go to the wedding because there would be a ton of people from high school I hadn't seen in a while, plenty

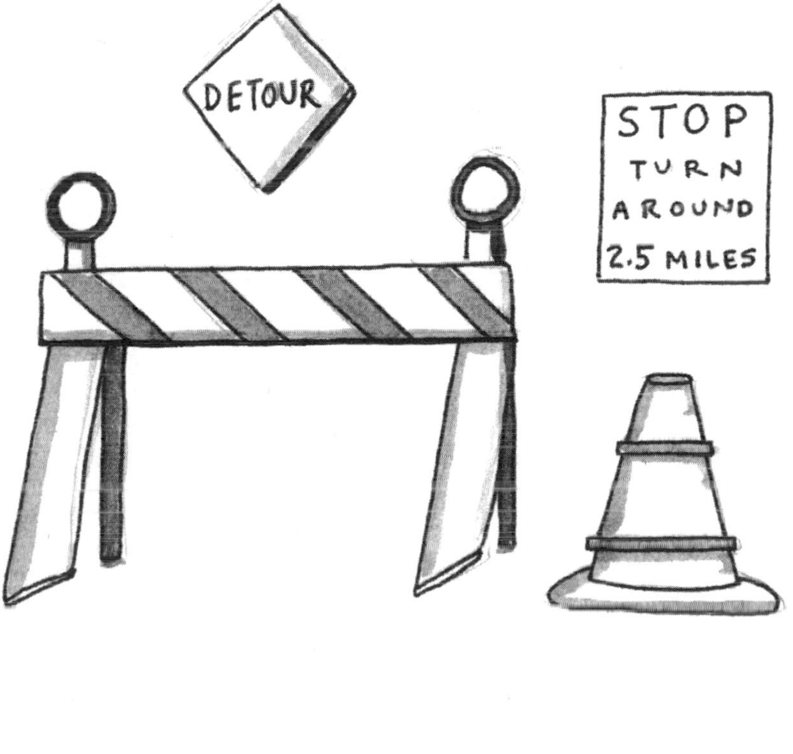
DETOUR
STOP
TURN
AROUND
2.5 MILES

of people I didn't know, and other fears both very reasonable (*What if I look silly dancing?*) and anxiety induced (*What if I'm so awful no one wants to talk to me?*). But Katie and I have been friends since childhood and grew up on the same street, so of course I wanted to be there when she got married at the Brookfield Zoo. It was just a matter of putting aside my own anxieties for the evening—a task that requires serious focus.

Unfortunately, the universe had other plans for me. The Chicago traffic was thick and congested, and I found myself cursing under my breath at every red light. I was met with unexpected construction and detours, which proved the old adage that "Chicago has only two seasons: winter and construction." This was followed by the horrible realization that I had no idea where I was going. By the time I got to the right parking lot, took a tram across the park, and started to walk to the ceremony, I was late. I began walking faster, heart thumping as I scurried in the right direction . . . only to realize I was hearing voices. Was the ceremony already starting? I quickly rounded the bend, but Katie and her fiancé, Kurt, were right in front of me, and I was facing the crowd.

I was walking smack into the altar.

This brings us to me hiding in the bushes, more embarrassed than I had ever been. I had been assigned one adult task—show up to my friend's wedding—and I'd failed spectacularly at that. My anxiety was in overdrive at this point, making my head swirl with thoughts about what an awful friend I was.

I hid behind the bushes until the ceremony was over and then attempted to seamlessly blend into the crowd. Maybe no one would notice I hadn't been at the actual wedding. The guests made their way to the cocktail hour, and I was hanging out by the polar bear tank when Katie's mother approached me. My heart sank when she asked me what I thought of the ceremony. It all came spilling out.

She just said, "Beth, calm down. This is Katie and Kurt's day. We all want Katie to have a good time, but if you bring up how you were late and missed parts of the ceremony, it could upset her. Just let it go, focus on having a good time, and enjoy yourself. Because we are all here to have a good time!"

Katie's mom was absolutely right. This day was a celebration of Katie and Kurt—not a celebration of my anxiety. The best possible thing I could do for everyone right then was to enjoy myself, even if that seemed like a monumental task.

I was going to be the best damn wedding guest they'd ever seen.

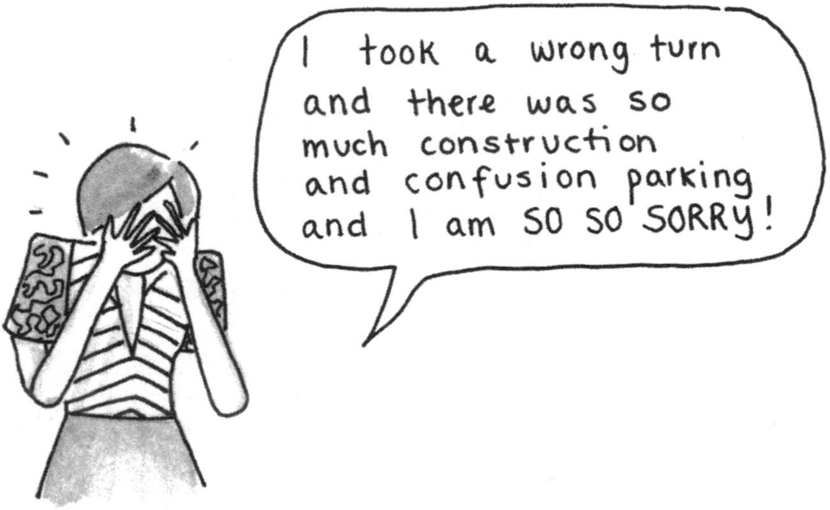
I took a wrong turn and there was so much construction and confusion parking and I am SO SO SORRY!

You're here now, so relax and celebrate - if Katie sees you upset, <u>she</u> will be upset, and neither of us wants that. So enjoy yourself and have fun!

At dinner I stepped out of my comfort zone, making sure I talked to everyone at my table. I asked questions, and answered the ones people posed to me. Rapid-fire conversation took place, and I continued to ignore the sinking feeling of being late to the wedding. I wore a smile on my face, but after a while it didn't even feel like pretending, because I was actually having fun. My stomach wasn't doing somersaults every five seconds. The people were easy to talk to, and everyone laughed at my uncool jokes. I was making progress, and no one even asked if I had seen the ceremony.

But to really be a good guest, I was going to have to dance. I had been at Katie's house earlier in the week, and everyone had teased me about not dancing, which embarrassed me a bit. But a good guest partakes in events, and dancing was certainly an event. So I dragged myself out on the floor and tried to do some goofy moves. As the songs kept getting better and better, I soon found it effortless to keep dancing. In fact, I actually *liked* it. I danced with everyone around me, chatting and screaming along to the songs. At one point it was just me on the dance floor, doing embarrassing moves to a-ha's "Take on Me." When Katie's mom saw that I was dancing and happy, she smiled at me from her spot by the wall.

The most unexpected turn of the night came when Katie

threw her bridal bouquet. Tradition dictates that the single girls line up, and whoever catches the flowers is supposed to be the next one to marry. I've been to a few weddings but never really paid much attention to this. We all got dragged out onto the floor, and I took my place in the group of girls.

The bouquet went flying into the air . . .

. . . and I caught it.

It was a whirlwind; all of a sudden everyone stepped away from me and I stood alone on the dance floor, lights spinning around me, holding the flowers while the crowd screamed and cheered. I felt elated, and Katie gave me a big hug. The photographer took our picture, and I looked down at the flowers. Surely traditions don't mean anything real, right?

The next song was slower, and I stood in the doorway holding my flowers. One of the groomsmen came and asked me to dance. He was very tall and I'm not so tall, so I kind of just held the thumb of his giant hand. I wanted to go back in time and tell my past self that eventually, nights wouldn't just be for crying under blankets and feeling like the world was swallowing me whole—sometimes I'd get to dance with boys at weddings.

When the night wound down and it was time to leave, I rode the tram through the now pitch-black zoo. Distant ani-

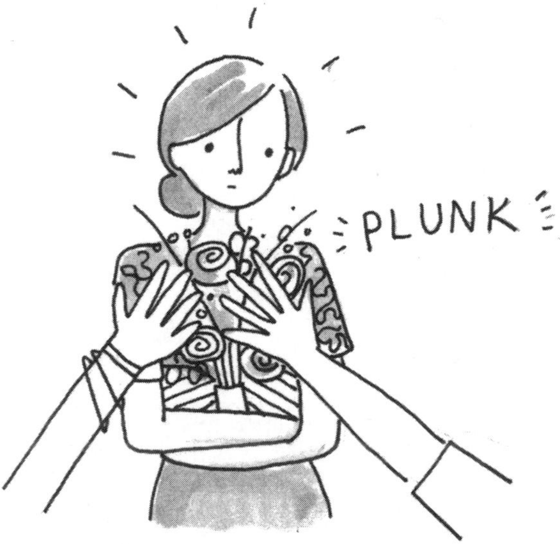
PLUNK

mal noises kept all the sleepy party guests awake, and I looked at the bouquet again. Maybe the flowers signaled that I would commit myself to someone else in the future, or maybe they signaled that I'm committed to working on my anxieties and that I had made ample progress that night.

Either way, they smelled fresh and sweet, with a hint of the future.

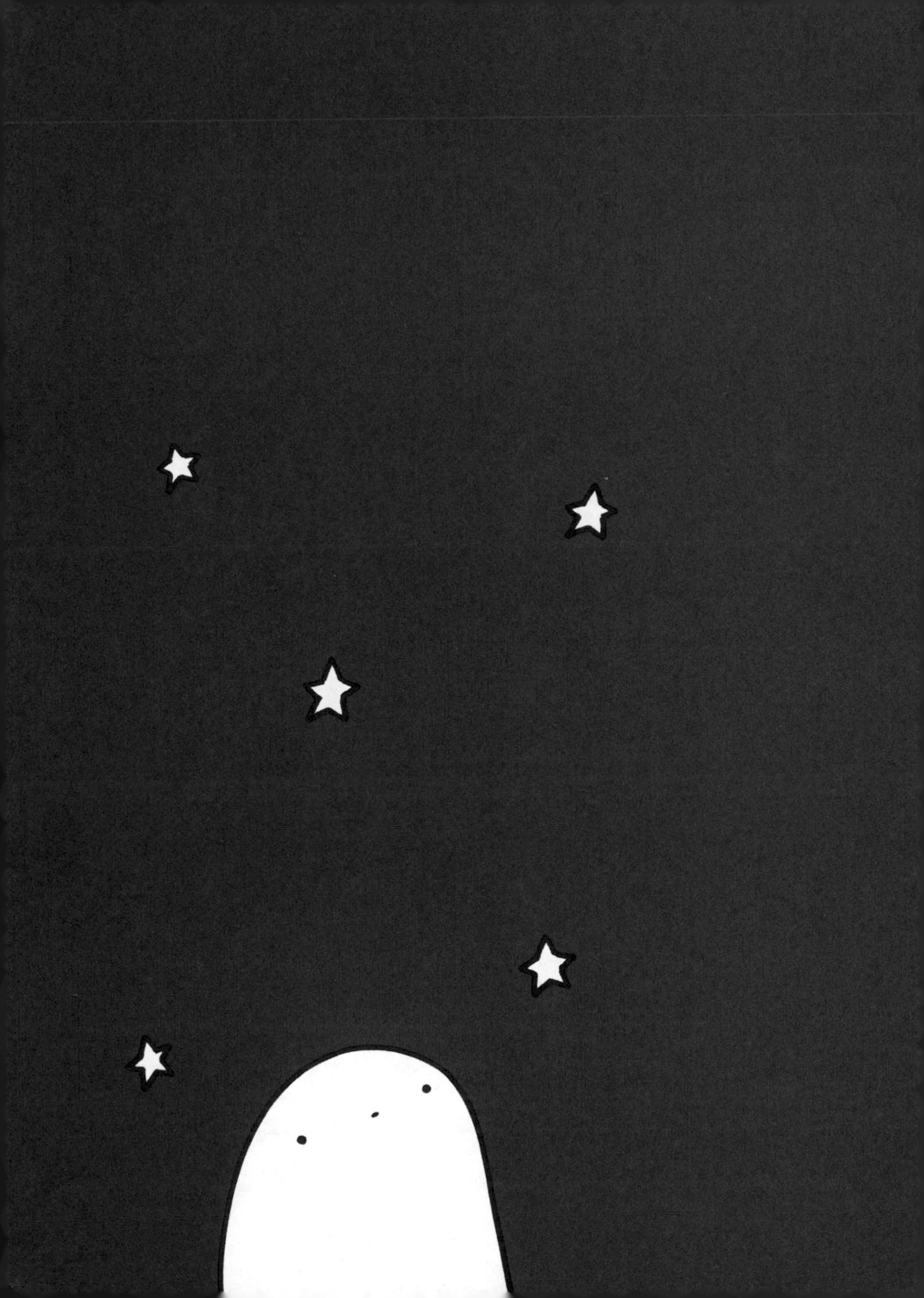

Acknowledgments

I'd like to thank Liate Stehlik and Jennifer Hart, Cassie Jones, Susan Kosko, Leah Carlson-Stanisic, Jeanne Reina, Jeanie Lee, Molly Waxman, Julie Paulauski, Caitlin Garing, and everyone at William Morrow and HarperCollins who helped me turn this book from an impossible dream into a reality.

Additionally, I'd like to especially thank Emma Brodie, my editor, who read all my terrible drafts, laughed at my stupid jokes, sent me romance novels, and became a friend in the process. Words will never fully describe how wonderful you are.

Special thanks to Penny Moore and Andrea Barzvi at Empire Literary, who answered all my ridiculous questions, saw potential in me when I couldn't see any for myself, and are overall two of the best people I have ever met. I'd also like to thank Sandy Hodgman for arranging the foreign rights and giving me a crash course in tax forms and being endlessly patient with me.

It would also be nice to thank Eli, my best friend, who was endlessly enthusiastic, read all my comics, and suggested I thank Danny DeVito in her place. Thanks to Brittany and Krystal, who read all of my goofy text messages and provided support. Elisabeth, my twelve-point friend from Austria, and Ruby, my *Black Books*–misery pal—both of you have been such fantastic internet friends. Extra thanks to Cody, my therapist, for all the insight and for letting me kick my shoes off in the chair.

I'd also like to thank my mom and dad—thanks for letting me crash at your place.

Lastly, thank you to everyone who read my work over the years. The continued support, encouraging messages, and interest in my comics have been phenomenal. Your readership has meant the world to me; thank you for making this the first book I didn't have to make by hand.

About the Author

BETH EVANS is an illustrator and comic artist with more than 270,000 followers across various social media platforms. She likes keeping up on Instagram, Twitter, and Tumblr as a means to share her insightful humor with the world. Beth lives in the Chicago area and enjoys wearing oversize pajamas while drawing comics that capture hard-to-describe feelings on a daily basis. She is the illustrator for *Breaking Mad* by Anna Williamson, which hit #1 on Amazon UK. Her work has appeared across media outlets from HuffPost to Buzzfeed to MSNBC.